Getting a Life;
Making a Living

How to Start and Run Your Own Business

A simple course guide for the
first-time entrepreneur

Alice Elliott Brown

A Publication in The Master-of-My-Universe Series

Pergados Press
Gainesville, Virginia

This book is informational, educational, and entertaining. The author and publisher expressly disclaim responsibility for any adverse effects arising from the use or application of information contained in this book.

www.AliceElliottBrown.com

email: Publisher@AliceElliottBrown.com

Print Edition: DriveZero, an imprint of Pergados Press.

ISBN-10: 0-9725368-6-8

ISBN-13: 978-0-9725368-6-8

Library of Congress Control Number: 2011900940

Printed in the United States of America

Dedication
This book is for all the people who get up in the
morning and dread going to work. May you find
the strength to follow your bliss and live your
dream.

Whether you think you can, or whether you think you can't,
you're right.
---- Henry Ford

Contents

Introduction, *p. 1*

Module 1: Planning, *p. 5*
    1-1: Selecting a product
    1-2: Identifying your market
    1-3: Projecting sales
    1-4: Estimating costs
    1-5: Defining cash needs
    1-6: Writing the business plan

Module 2: Funding, *p. 41*
    2-1: Sources of cash
    2-2: Debt vs equity
    2-3: About vulture capital
    2-4: The perils of taking money from friends
    2-5: Mortgaging your house
    2-6: Shoestrings and bootstraps

Module 3: Structuring, *p. 69*
    3-1: Choosing a legal structure
    3-2: Filing with the government
    3-3: Branding your company
    3-4: Hiring yourself and others
    3-5: Setting up your website
    3-6: Establishing your accounting system

Module 4: Marketing, *p. 107*
    4-1: Reaching your target customer
    4-2: Launching your product
    4-3: Differentiating your offering
    4-4: Erecting competitive barriers
    4-5: Nurturing your competence
    4-6: Milking social media

Module 5: Operating, *p. 137*

5-1: Offices and equipment
5-2: Staff
5-3: Inventory
5-4: Customer relationships
5-5: Accounting
5-6: Strategic relevance

Module 6: Growing and exiting, *p. 165*

6-1: Managing cash and growth
6-2: Developing people
6-3: Monitoring your reputation
6-4: Choosing your successor
6-5: Selling your business
6-6: Living the life you've dreamed

Module 7: Getting a Life, *p. 193*

Introduction – About Getting a Life

If you've dreamed of running your own business, you may have looked for a simple guide about the basic facts. You may have wanted a simple "How-to" book. In your search, you may have noticed that textbooks on entrepreneurship focus on theory, not practice. They give you ideas and concepts, when you are looking for instructions. As most small business managers know, experience is the best teacher. Jumping right in and running your own business is the best way to learn. In this course, we will focus only on the practical aspects of "getting it done." We will give you the website URLs for the Internal Revenue Service's practical pages. We will direct you to the state corporation commissions' forms to incorporate. We will explain how to issue your own direct corporate stock. We will show you how to forecast a cash budget to apply for loans.

The unemployment rate is soaring. If you've lost your job, you can print up some business cards and call yourself a consultant. You can search your inventory of talents, and find some skill to offer. You can crash a trade show and hand out your business cards to the paying attendees. When you do that, and someone offers to buy what you are selling, you are in business for yourself. After you have been in business for yourself, you may never choose to go back to being an employee. The thrill and the freedom of entrepreneurship are addictive.

You might be scared to take the plunge, though. Maybe you are worried no one will take you up on your offer. Maybe you wonder if anyone will buy what you sell. Maybe you think you will make a mistake, run out of cash, or miss a credit card payment. Maybe you think you need a lawyer to set things up for you.

Maybe you think entrepreneurs work day and night and never take a vacation.

Maybe you think you're not good enough to run a business.

Maybe you're wondering if it's possible to enjoy your life, while running a business. Then again, maybe you are working long hours in a tedious and unsatisfying job right now. Maybe you wonder if it's possible for anybody to get a life, while making a living.

Many entrepreneurs say yes, you must be both passionate and obsessive to build your business successfully. Others say passion is required, but a balanced life of family, community, spirit, and work produces the most satisfaction. Still others say, what is success? Who defines it but yourself? If you can make a living from your business, pay your bills, reduce your stress, and feel inner satisfaction from your work, what is more successful than that? What good does it do to be considered successful by others, but feel miserable and empty inside? How many Hollywood celebrities end up in rehab on suicide watch? We think they have it all, and they think suicide is the best option. Success is defined by our own standards. This applies to your successful business, too.

Unless you were born with a trust fund, you are probably going to work for a living. That work will occupy most of your waking hours. It will take your time, and as Benjamin Franklin told us, "time is what life is made of." How can we pursue happiness and enjoy life, when our life is filled with an exhausting, tedious, boring, and demeaning job?

Now maybe you have a great job and you love what you do. If so, maybe you think you could do your job better if you owned the company. You need some insight and some facts, to start your own company.

Maybe you are an artist, designer, musician, or writer. You go to work at a mundane job, to make money to pay the bills. You want to make a living doing creative work, but you don't know how to manage the business. You don't know the rules, you don't like rules on general principles, and you don't know how to begin. Maybe you are thinking you could manage your creative career if you had a simple guidebook to business.

Maybe your goals are not so lofty. You just want to support your family through your own effort. You'd like to open a neighborhood grocery, an ethnic restaurant, a beauty salon, or a local gym. You want step-by-step instructions.

There are two basic types of business start-ups. The type we most often think about is the Big Dream. This is the one where your company's growth explodes, you get venture capital investment, you get listed on the stock market, and you become a billionaire. This one is not likely to happen.

The second type of business is the attractive venture. It's the local dry-cleaner, florist shop, landscape business, or caterer. It's the small business serving a neighborhood. It will never go public. It's owner will continue to work in this business every day. Its advantage is that it pays the bills for the owner's family. It allows the owner to both get a life and pay the bills.

Whatever your goals for starting your business, you need to know the rules of the game. *Getting a Life; Making a Living* tells you the rules. It's the set of directions that comes in the gamebox. After you read the directions, playing the game is up to you.

If you are thinking of starting your own business, and need some help with practical basics, this handbook will skip the philosophy. It will go straight to the facts of what to do. The handbook is set up so that you can take each lesson in an evening after work. Come home, have dinner, sit down at the computer. Instead of checking your Facebook page, surf over to AliceElliottBrown.com and spend an hour with the evening's lesson in business. Play around with the exercises. Try your hand at the quizzes. Post a comment on the blog. Meet others who share your interests. Maybe it will help you put those pieces together to strike out on your own, in your own business.

Can't find a job? Why not hang out your shingle and go it alone? Isn't small business the basic building block of the American Way? When you learn more about business, that knowledge will help you choose the next step in your career. Whatever this course does for you, you will know more when it's over. There are no tests to submit or hurdles to jump. No one will grade your work, or criticize your performance. This class is for you to use to learn. It's your tool, for your advancement. You decide whether it helps you, and you decide how well you are doing. No judgment will be involved.

In your universe, you are the Master. Let this set of lessons on business be just another arrow in your quiver, another tool in your toolbox, and another valuable skill in your bank of assets.

To do the quizzes online, navigate to http://www.AliceElliottBrown.com/ Select "Take business classes here" from the left menu. The lessons are best done in order, beginning with Module 1. There is no registration, no login, no information or identification required. Just push the buttons and do your thing.

But, if you'd like . . .
send me an email at AliceElliottBrown@RiverLandingPress.com and let me know what you think...Best wishes for your future success,

Alice Elliott Brown

Module 1: Planning

1-1: Selecting a product
1-2: Identifying your market
1-3: Projecting sales
1-4: Estimating costs
1-5: Defining cash needs
1-6: Writing the business plan

Module 1:Planning
Lesson 1: Selecting a product

Use your weirdness, How to select a product that will sell, Identify possibilities, Testing the market.

Most business books will tell you to start your business by analyzing the market.   *The market for what?* Your best bet to run a successful business is to base it on something which you, and only you, have to sell. *Uniquely.* There is something about you that is a valuable asset, which other people would agree to buy.   Whether it is the Magic card collection you started in the fourth grade, your ability to identify wild herbs, your passion for crossword puzzles, or your uncanny talent in playing World of Warcraft, the business you are going to start will be based on something about *you* that is very special. After all, you are going to put a lot of time and effort into this business.   It has to be about something that has meaning and reward for you personally.

Use your weirdness
Do not tell yourself there is nothing special about you.   You are special, in some weird, unusual way. If you can't think of it, ask your best friend what it is.   There are at least two, and maybe as many as six, ways that you are unique, odd, outstanding, unusual, or just plain weird. It is your weirdness that will be your primary asset in defining your business plan. Think about it. We each have talents and abilities of some type, even though they may not fit into conventional society.   Some part of your special talents will be the basis of your business. That's what will give you your competitive advantage. It is why you will be the unchallenged "boss" of this business. It is what will make your future employees refer to you as "the genius." It is what will turn your flaws into your features. Business theory refers to this as your "distinctive competence." In a competitive industry, you need a distinctive competence: something you do better than anybody else can do.   You conceive the idea for your business, based around your personal distinctive competence.

This causes you to be the person who is standing in the right place at the right time. Building a business around your personal talent makes you appear to be lucky. No matter how odd your interests are, there is a special set, or "niche," of other people who are odd just like you! You don't need *everybody* to want your product. You just need to be able to find the niche of special people who do want it.

How do you select a product that will sell?
Of course, the product you offer must be one that someone wants to buy. The first task is to identify all the possible products for which you might have a unique advantage. From that list, we will look at each one and test whether it might have a market. Write down what you do to relax and have fun. What pleases you and makes you feel energized? Do you like to play music, listen to music, play computer games, shop, give parties, garden, argue about politics, cook fancy dinners, travel, collect rocks, do puzzles, read novels, or work with your hands in a woodshop? Do you like to play soccer, watch football, set off fireworks, make quilts, take photographs, or draw caricatures? Whatever it is that you like to do in your "spare" time, be assured that there are other people who are like you. Those other people who like to do what you like to do are the people you will soon be calling your "customers." Write as many different things down as you can. Whatever interests you, whatever you enjoy doing, write it on your list.

> *Example: Bob likes to hike, play soccer, and listen to classical music. He also went to Hawaii one year, and he'd like to go back. Janice likes to build scrapbooks with memorabilia from important events in her life. Marcia likes to sing karaoke and cook outdoors on the grill with a lot of friends. Jerry likes to fix old clocks. Ellen likes to make pottery. Joe likes to play ball with his dog.*

Whatever it is, it is. Just write on your list some things that you like to do. It's okay to put on there something that you think you would like to do, but you have never actually done. For example, maybe you think you would like to travel to India, but you've never done it. If it is something you have been thinking about for a long time, and it interests you, put it on the list.

Identify the possibilities

After you have your list of things you like to do and things that interest you, next take each of those things and make another list under each one. Call this new list "products." For each of the activities you like to do, list all the products and services which you use and pay for while you are doing that activity. Let your mind roam freely. Think about products and services to make your activity more enjoyable. Maybe those products and services don't exist yet. If they did exist, you would buy them. If you can think of a service you would like to have, but it doesn't exist, put that on your list, too. List as many types of products and services as you can.

> *Example: When Bob goes hiking, he uses maps, backpacks, walking sticks, hiking shoes and socks, flashlights, compasses, a digital camera, and water bottles. He also drives to a national park, where he talks to the guide about the different trails. Once a year, he participates in a group hiking experience, where the group plans a trip to different parks around the country. They stay overnight and use a service to deliver their supplies to their destination.*

Look at your list of possible products. Think about any other products or services that you would like to use, if they existed, but that don't exist. Then take each of your products and think about what you could do to supply that product, or a better, improved version of that product, to other people who like to do what you do. Think about what you would have to do to become a supplier of each product.

> *Example: Bob considered that he could make walking sticks by hand. He had made his own walking sticks before, and liked the ones he made. He also considered setting up a service to review the trails he had explored, and*

providing information to other hikers about the trails and nearby towns and services for planning their trips. He also had a nice portfolio of photographs from his trips, and wondered if they could be of any value. Additionally, Bob noticed that the water bottle he was using came from China. He wondered if there would be any way he could improve on the weight and shape of the bottle. There was also a problem on his trips that he would like to solve: getting fresh water along the trail. Armed with this set of problems to be solved, Bob was ready to move on to testing the market.

Testing the market

Bob's product selection is not yet complete. He made the first draft of his product selection. It is his "strawman." His product is not just walking sticks. Walking sticks are easy to buy or make. His product is a handmade, specially-designed walking stick, which comes from the guy who posts those beautiful pictures about trails, and blogs about each of the special aspects of the trails, and has an idea for a great new water solution. His product includes not just the walking stick, but the "branding" of that walking stick as a special solution to a hikers' unique problems and interests. The walking stick, because it is associated with the additional information which Bob provides, will have more value than a standard walking stick. The association with Bob's name is called "branding." Branding adds value and makes it possible to get higher prices.

You, too, need a first draft of your product selection. Your "strawman" product gives you something to throw darts at, while you are refining your ability to hit the bullseye on the target market. This product selection will be an iterative process. Choose something. Test the market for it. Refine your choice. Test the market again. Throw a lot up against the wall and see what sticks. When you start getting a response from people, then, *and only then*, you have found your product.

Key points:
   1. *The product you sell must be something you enjoy and understand.*
   2. *Other people who have your same interest are your target market. Everyone doesn't have to like your product. You only need a specialized interest segment, called a "niche."*
   3. *You must refine your product idea by testing whether it appeals to your target market.*

Next lesson: Module 1: Planning, Lesson 2: Identifying your market

Module 1: Planning
Lesson 2: Identifying your market

Definition of a niche market, Market research, Reaching your target audience, "Push vs pull" marketing, The four P's of the market mix.

You've selected your initial set of product ideas. You've chosen a general concept for your business, based on your personal assets, interests, and idiosyncracies. Your business concept revolves around something which is particularly meaningful for you, based on who you are. It is something you will enjoy spending most of your waking hours doing. If you are going to be happy with your business, the business concept must be personally enjoyable to you. You will put serious effort into this business. It is important to want to spend your time at this activity. Having chosen the main concept of your business, you will refine that concept to fit the market.

Often, people think they have to choose a big market. No, your market can be quite small, as long as you are able to access it. You need to be able to find the people who are interested. You must capture and defend a significant share of your market. That is, if the market for Bob's Walking Sticks is 500 walking sticks per year, then Bob's goal is to get the biggest share of those 500 walking sticks. If Bob can dominate a small, narrowly defined market, he can protect his pricing and his brand. His only concern is whether he can reach the people who are interested in buying walking sticks, at the time they are looking to buy, with a message which triggers the purchase. As a small company, it is more realistic for Bob to project that he can get a 50% market share of walking sticks, or 250 walking sticks per year, than it is for Bob to project that he can get a 1% market share of something which is a much larger market. It is more likely that you can dominate a small, specialized market, than it is that you can capture a tiny portion of a large market.

Definition of a "niche" market

A small, specialized set of customers with the same interest is called a niche. Your goal, as a small business person, is to pick your niche market, and dominate it. You must be the best provider of something that is special and unique. Every person who is interested in the special characteristics of your product needs to hear your message, and you need to be able to find those people to sell to them. The question you must answer first is: given the basic product concept I have identified, who are the people who care about that product? What are they looking for? What features do they want in this product? What causes them to decide to buy? How much will they be willing to pay? What alternatives do they have to buy this same product from other companies? What substitutes for this product do they use now?

> *In the example of Bob's Walking Sticks, Bob knows a lot about people who hike as a hobby. He understands how they plan their trips, what intrigues them about a walking stick, and why they would buy one. Based on Bob's personal knowledge of other hikers, he concludes that the buyer of his walking stick cares about the environment, values craftsmanship and artistry, and wants a functional stick made of solid wood, and sized to the hiker's height and weight. He believes his target customer will be willing to pay $65 for a hiking stick, at retail prices. He also believes that a smaller part of his market will be willing to pay $130 for a hiking stick, if the stick has high quality carvings and a compass attached.*

Of course, at this point, that is just Bob's guess. He doesn't know whether he is right or wrong. He will test his theories by asking some people what they think of his product idea. More importantly, he will need to know what it will take for people to buy his walking stick. He'll find out by asking them.

Market Research

You probably won't buy a market research report for your business. The reasonably good ones cost thousands of dollars. While some would argue that a decision like this requires a little money spent on research, you will get a better return on specific and direct research that is targeted exactly to your product. Canned reports, costing a few thousand dollars, will be directed to larger companies and generic products. You need, however, to do your own direct market research. One way you could do this is to make a prototype product. You will also want to use the social media aspects of the Internet to research your market. Bob entered "walking sticks" into Google, and tried to buy one. He looked for his competitors, checked e-Bay, searched for blogs and customer comments, and generally tried to get a map in his mind of the industry.

Bob made a few different walking sticks. He took them to his hiking group and asked his friends what they thought of them. He asked them what they would like to change about his product, and got them to talk about walking sticks, and why they would buy them. Bob listened carefully to his friends, and made some changes to his product. He understood that he would only be able to sell walking sticks to people who were serious about hiking as a hobby, and he determined to know everything he could about hikers and their concerns. Bob signed himself up for the RSS feeds[1] on every blog about hiking he could find. Bob wanted to know what his customers thought.

Reaching your target audience

There were magazines for hikers. There were hiking clubs. Both of those were possible ways to find his potential customers. Both of them would require very large amounts of money for

---

1

    RSS feeds: a subscription service which notifies you when changes and new posts are made to a website. It allows the Blog to contact you by email.

print advertising, in order to communicate his message. Bob concluded he could not spend that amount of money to advertise.

> Bob had selected a small, specialized, niche. Now he had to craft a message that would be meaningful to people who wanted to buy a high quality walking stick. He knew what his friends thought, but he wondered how he could find more people who were just like his friends. He had to figure out where people like him and his friends would go to look for walking sticks.

Fortunately for Bob, there was a media that would allow him to find people who wanted to learn more about hiking. Bob knew that people who were interested in hiking would be typing "hiking" into a search engine on the Internet. All Bob had to do was make sure that when people typed "hiking" into Google, they found his landing page to sell walking sticks. It had to come up on the first page, and it had to sound like the right link to click to get good information. That's when Bob realized his success in selling walking sticks would depend on becoming the best provider of information about hiking on the Internet.

Finding and reaching his target customers suddenly became something Bob would be able to do, with very little investment of money, but very much investment of his time and effort. He realized that the key success factor for his business would be his website, and its position in search engines, along with its credibility as a source of information. His walking sticks had to be high quality, yes. The quality of his product, however, would be a necessary but not sufficient condition for success. Given that he had a good product, and given that it met the need of a specific type of customer, Bob would succeed if and only if he could provide a website that would be found by his target audience.

"Push" vs "Pull" marketing

In the old days, marketing textbooks would tell you there were two types of marketing. You could "push" the product, meaning you would send salesmen door to door, make telemarketing calls, put ads in magazines, buy television commercials, and get a spot on the television shopping channel. All of this activity was meant to generate "pull." In pull marketing, the customer walks into a retail store and asks for the product. Once they are pushed into the store, they are pulled to buy through in-store discounts and display ads. Print advertising, telemarketers, direct sales people, and television commercials cost a lot.

Today, however, people who want to buy something will research it on the Internet first. The key is, you have to be found when they are looking, and provide the information they need. When they search, you have to come up in the search results on the first page. Additionally, you have to get customers talking about you to their friends. They will do that on the social networking sites.

Product, Place, Promotion, and Price

This is the standard of marketing advice. You have to have the right product, offered in the right physical location, presented with the right promotional message, and sold at the right price. The word "right" means "acceptable to the target buyer." In these days, the "Place" is the Internet. While people may not buy on the Internet, they will definitely research on the Internet before buying. You have to get placed in the search engines so that you will be found with the right key words, or through word of mouth by email or social networking sites such as Facebook and MySpace. The "Promotion" is the message on your website, and the argument for buying which those who land on your site perceive. Price and Product are still valid concerns. Your product must meet the needs of a potential set of customers, at a price that offers value to them, in a place where they can find you using key words, and with a message that resonates for them.

The key to sales revenue is the buyer's mindset.   You must present a message to a potential buyer, at the time when they are looking to solve a problem, with a product that can solve it, for a price which represents value to them.   Even further, you must deliver on the promise of your marketing message.   Your customers will first search the Internet to compare your offering to their substitute options.   There, they will find comments from customers who have tried your product.   If the experience of other customers was not positive, you will lose the sale.

If you can find a way to present your message to potential buyers, at the time they are looking for a solution to a problem, with a solution which they perceive to be valuable, and which delivers on its promises, you have the potential to develop a successful business which will support your family and provide you with a quality lifestyle.

Key points:
1. *You must select a narrowly defined niche market and pursue market share dominance.*
2. *Your customers have alternatives. You must provide an option which they perceive to be the best value.*
3. *Your target market is talking on the Internet. You can find them there and ask what they want.*
4. *You have to deliver on your marketing promise. Your customers will continue to talk after the sale.*
5. *You must be in the place where your customer is looking for a solution to the problem you solve. You must be there at the time the customer is looking.*
6. *You cannot be a solution looking for a problem. If you have no competitors, you have no market.*

Next lesson: Module 1: Planning, Lesson 3: Projecting Sales

Module 1: Planning
Lesson 3: Projecting Sales

Start with the price, Build a product line, More than viable, The sales goals depend on the life goals, Cash is not profit.

In Lesson 2, we said the key is the buyer. We said "You must present a message to a potential buyer, at the time when they are looking to solve a problem, with a product that can solve it, for a price which represents value to them."

> *Bob asked his friends how much they would pay for his Super-Deluxe Artistic Walking Stick with a compass attached. Most of the 100 people in his hiking club said they already had a walking stick, so they wouldn't pay anything. Ten people said they would pay $35. Fifteen people said they would pay $45. Four people said they would pay $50, if they could choose which design was carved in it. One person said, "Does that compass give me my GPS coordinates? Because if it does, I would pay $120 for it." As a result of his survey, Bob can now guess that the market for walking sticks is now 30 people out of every 100 people who belong to a hiking club. He knows that most of those people will pay between $35 and $50, but a few of those people will pay $120, provided there are enhanced features, like a GPS system. Bob also knows that every person who goes hiking does not belong to a hiking club, so he considers his survey to be conservative and modest. He believes the market is larger than just hiking club members, but he is not sure how large.*

Bob felt disappointed. He had hoped to price his product at $65. Now, he realized this would not work. He knew he had to lower his sales revenue projection. He needed to re-estimate how many walking sticks he could sell.

Bob could attempt to estimate the size of the market by looking for published statistics about hikers. However, he isn't going to spend any time doing that. Bob's time is valuable, and he knows the numbers he would come up with for market size would not change his next action. Time management is important for an aspiring entrepreneur, so Bob tries not to do things that will not make a difference in his decision-making. Bob is willing to skip the estimate of market size. He's convinced the uncertainty in his estimates would make the number unreliable. In his research, he realized that a high-end walking stick would be a unique product. Instead of estimating overall market size, Bob is wondering how many sales he would need in order to meet his own goal of providing an income for his family from selling walking sticks. Once he figures that out, he will try to judge whether the market is big enough to meet his needs.

Start with the price

Bob didn't figure out his costs, add a profit, and call that his price. Bob knows that price is a measure of value in the eyes of the buyer. He knows people will decide what a product is worth to them, and that is all they will pay. He knows his question is: given the value of a walking stick to its buyer, can they be produced with a reasonable margin? Bob has many options to structure the cost of his product. He could make tradeoffs in those options, in order to meet the price point of the potential buyers.

> *Tip: In projecting sales for your product, you have to make a guess about what people will pay. Asking people is an excellent way to find out. Sometimes, you may have to make just one or two prototype products, and ask people to tell you what they would consider a good value. Their opinions are not the final decision. They give a clue about how to choose the price point, not an answer.*

Build a product "line"

For most products, there can be multiple versions for different segments of the market. There may be people who care only about cost, and want to buy the cheapest possible model that does the job. Other people may care about the artistic elements. Still others may care about added features and benefits. You can start out with only one product version, and add others as you learn more about the buyers. For each of your product lines, you will estimate sales for that version, compared to production costs.

> *Bob thinks he will sell most of his walking sticks in the $40 range. He is planning to make a "plain" version that is simple to produce for that segment of his market. He also wants to make a "fancy" version. He is going to put a simple GPS system on the top of it. He knows a place in China where he can buy one at a low price. He's going to try to sell that version for $130.*

In truth, Bob has no idea how many of each of these he can sell. He doesn't have the experience or the data to even make a responsible guess. So at this point in his planning process, Bob is going to use a "plug number" for his projected sales. That means, Bob is going to set up a spreadsheet with a line item on it that says Total Sales by month. Then, Bob is going to figure out what it will cost him to build each of his product versions. He is going to place his cost numbers on the spreadsheet.

After that, Bob is going to "plug in" the number of sales he would have to make in each product line before he would get to a "breakeven." That is, he is going to calculate how many products have to be sold to recover his costs. When Bob knows the number of products necessary to cover his costs, then, and only then, will he assess whether or not the market will bear that level of product sales.

For example, if his calculation says he will have to sell more walking sticks than there are members in all the hiking clubs of the United States, then Bob will probably conclude that walking sticks are not a viable business. On the other hand, if his breakeven calculation says that he only has to sell enough walking sticks to provide 1 stick for every 100 members of hiking clubs in the U S, then Bob will think he may have a viable business. It's a judgment call which every entrepreneur makes. Bob's research will include learning how many hiking enthusiasts could be reached by his marketing efforts. His target market must be identifiable and reachable. He must know *who* they are and *where* they can be contacted.

More than viable

Of course, Bob doesn't want to work hard at a business just to breakeven. He has to be sure the market for walking sticks, and his own potential sales in that market, will be enough to cover a salary for him that can support his family. If it does that, he will begin to be interested in this business. Bob has higher goals, too. He doesn't want to just scrape by. He wants the business to provide savings for his future, health insurance for his family, college for his kids, vacations in Antigua, and a car of his choosing. Bob is going to estimate those costs, and add them to his spreadsheet. Then he is going to go back to his "Total Sales" line, and plug in a new number. This will tell him how many walking sticks he must sell to provide a nice lifestyle for himself. If that number also turns out to be a reasonable and possible, in Bob's personal judgment, he will continue to consider this business. If Bob sees that there is no pot of gold at the end of this rainbow, he will stop chasing it.

The sales goals depend on the life goals

If Bob's dream were to build a multi-million dollar business and expand globally, putting a walking stick in every garage, he might conclude that the market would not sustain a sales volume high enough to meet his goals. He might modify his product offering. Maybe he would expand his business idea to fitness centers, or to retail stores specializing in hiking and outdoor clothing and paraphernalia. Even without market research reports, Bob can make a personal guess about whether or not his product can become a worldwide phenomenon. Entrepreneurs guess wrong all the time, but they keep guessing. The key to successful guessing is to try a little, test the waters, notice and pay attention to the customer feedback. The successful entrepreneur changes the approach to respond to customers, and tries again. The more Bob fails, the more he learns. He sees failure as a new opportunity to change his actions and get it right next time. In this case, Bob isn't interested in building a major corporation. His desire for entrepreneurship revolves around his choice to live a certain lifestyle. He doesn't want to risk his life savings, worry about meeting payroll, or travel to visit his factory in Malaysia. Some entrepreneurs do want to do that, but Bob doesn't. Bob's sales projections will be limited by his goals. He wants to have enough to run an attractive small business. He does not want to run a global manufacturing enterprise. Bob's projected sales, then, derive from the amount of money Bob needs to live his dream. They do not project endlessly up. It's a good thing, too. You see, if your business is growing quickly, your business is cash poor. The faster you grow, the higher your need for investment.

Cash is not profit

The higher the investment needs, the more "moral hazard" for you. You may be asked to sell your integrity, your deepest convictions, and figuratively your first-born child, in order to get the money. If you have a lot of debt, you will have a lot of worry. Cash is a serious subject, to the entrepreneur. It is much more serious and important than that fuzzy and illusory, taxable cousin: profit. Cash and profit are two different concepts. The entrepreneur is keenly aware of the difference.

Key points:
1. *Price is a measure of value in the eyes of the buyer. The product line offers different strokes for different folks. It lets your customers make choices and tradeoffs.*
2. *Before you chase a rainbow, check to see if there is a pot of gold at the end of it.*
3. *We learn from our failures and try again – but we try differently each time. We don't fail the same way twice.*
4. *Cash is not profit.*

Next lesson: Module 1: Planning, Lesson 4: Estimating Costs

Module 1: Planning
Lesson 4: Estimating Costs

Identifying elements of cost, Fixed vs variable costs, Determining breakeven

Everything we do in business planning is iterative and temporary. We project sales based on a goal. When the goals change, the sales projections change. When the sales projections change, the cost estimates change. This causes the cash needs to change. As the business progresses, we get more information about the behavior of customers. With this new information, our sales projections are re-assessed, basing them less on wishful thinking and more on history. Our projections improve as we remake them. Business planning is constant; we continually update our "guesses" as we receive better data. Even our costs change, as suppliers change their pricing to us. It is important that we understand, then, the assumptions made in our planning. Otherwise, we will not know how to update them when the context changes. Context changes because customers change. Their preferences, their demographics, and their environment change. They change their minds.

Some small business managers wonder why we make a business plan, when it is constantly changing. The reason is simple: the business plan is the rudder of the business. A small change in direction of the rudder causes the boat to ultimately end up in a very different place.   The business plan guides management actions and coordinates the team effort. Some textbooks call the business plan a map. The world of new product marketing has no map. It's uncharted territory. You set sail. You test the wind. You check your moral compass. You adjust the rudder. You constantly reassess the environment to stay on course.

Identifying Elements of Cost
The first step in estimating costs for your business plan is identifying what the elements of costs will be. You must truly

understand what it takes to produce your product or provide your service. Then you must understand what it takes to market and distribute your product. Finally, you will need to know what taxes, licenses, and regulations apply to your industry.

> *For example, in Bob's walking stick business, he lists the supplies he needs to make his product: small trees of a specified type and shape, varnish, paint, compasses, leather string, stones, shells, and feathers for decoration, rubber bottoms, glue.   Then he lists the equipment he needs: carving knives, a water tub to soften and remove the bark, hole punchers, glue gun.   Bob also needs a computer to keep his accounting records. He expects that he will need a marketing brochure, business cards, a purchased mailing list for hiking clubs and outdoor stores, and a separate telephone line for business. He also wants to get a website. He doesn't know how to make his own website, so Bob is going to budget to pay someone to make one for him.*

It takes time to make each walking stick. Bob currently makes each one himself, but he wants to plan for hiring employees to make them. In his plan, Bob will time himself making the sticks. He is going to record how long it takes him to do each step of the process, from finding the right trees in the woods behind his house, to tying the compasses onto the sticks with the leather string.   When he knows how long each task takes, he will consider how much he will have to pay to hire a person to do each task.   For example, if it takes him 5 minutes to pick up a compass and a leather string, make appropriate holes, and tie the compass onto the stick, Bob is planning to assign 5 minutes of labor at $X an hour, to each stick, for the task, "Tying on the compass." Bob will take each task and measure the amount of labor required, as part of his costing exercise.   With all of his cost elements identified, Bob will lay out a spreadsheet. He will divide the costs into "fixed costs" and "variable costs."

Fixed vs Variable Costs
On Bob's spreadsheet, he will divide his costs into Operations

costs, Marketing costs, and Administrative costs. Under administrative costs he will include a monthly fee for an accountant, and any license fees he will incur to run a business. To find out what fees he will need to run his business, Bob will go to the website for his state. He will search on "State Corporation Commission" for his state. It is likely that he will find out everything he needs to know about licenses and regulations for his business from the state website.

Before continuing onto his analysis of cash flow, Bob will divide up his Operations costs into "fixed costs", or those that will be incurred no matter how many sticks are made, and "variable costs," those that depend on the number of sticks produced. Some costs may be partly fixed and party variable. That is, they may provide a certain capacity and then have to be replaced. For example, Bob may need to buy a 5-gallon can of varnish. He may be able to produce 200 walking sticks with that 5-gallon can, but when he reaches walking stick number 201, he has to buy another 5-gallon can. Varnish isn't sold in 1 ounce packets, so Bob has to plan for the purchase of a 5-gallon can every 200 sticks.

Bob decides that his carving knives and other equipment are all fixed costs. Even though Bob already owns the equipment he needs, he is going to list that equipment on his spreadsheet as a cost of his business.   He will transfer ownership of that equipment to his business, and carry it as a business asset on his balance sheet. Because the county in which Bob lives taxes business equipment, he will be careful to transfer it at the appropriate cost for "used" equipment. In the future, when Bob buys new equipment with corporate funds, he will carefully note the price of the new equipment as a business capital cost.

Bob is going to take each cost element of producing a walking stick and assign it a "price per stick." This will become part of his "Cost of Goods Sold." He will calculate how much varnish he needs per stick, divide that into the cost of a 5-gallon can and assign that cost to the line item, "varnish." He will also calculate how much he has to pay for a person to tie the compasses onto the sticks. He will assign the five minutes of labor to each stick. When Bob has calculated all elements of a cost for each stick, he will list those elements and determine his variable "cost per stick."

Bob will list everything he has to spend to get his business started: from the cost of building his website to the cost of ordering business cards. He will list all his equipment needs and every penny he will spend to start the business. These are the costs that are "fixed." He will have to spend this money before he can sell his first walking stick.

Determining the "Breakeven"

With any new business, the entrepreneur has to carefully assess whether or not there is actually a pot of gold under the rainbow he or she is chasing. Bob knows, from his market research, how much people are willing to pay for a walking stick. Before he spends any money on his business, he has to evaluate whether or not he can make walking sticks at a price point that will allow him to make money. Not only does each walking stick have to make money, but it has to make enough money so that Bob can pay himself back for any cash he had to pay upfront to get the business started.

What Bob needs to know, before he spends any money on this business is this simple question: how many walking sticks do I have to sell before I get back my initial investment? Knowing that answer, Bob can then look at his own assessment of the size of the market, and make a judgment call about whether this business is going to be worth doing.

> Let's say Bob determines that he will need to spend $30,000 to get his business going. Most of that will be marketing costs and product launch activities. He will want to know, how soon can I get my $30,000 back? His calculation of product cost is $14 for each stick. He believes, based on his market surveys, that people will pay $40 for his stick. Bob

knows he will have to give the retail store and distributor half. This means he will get $20 for each stick. $20 - $14 is $6 in "contribution." So Bob knows that each stick nets $6 to contribute toward his business overhead and profit. This means he will have to sell 5,000 sticks to get his original investment back. ($30,000 divided by $6.)

Now Bob wonders . . . how long will it take for me to sell 5,000 walking sticks? If his answer is longer than six months, Bob will have to change his product idea. Why? Because Bob's goal is to support his family through this business, and he needs to be sure the numbers will prove that he can have a reasonable, if modest, income.

Other entrepreneurs may have different goals. As you see, the answers and the outcomes all tie back to the entrepreneur's goal.

Key point:

1. *The business plan is the rudder, not the roadmap. Small changes in direction cause the business to end up in a very different place.*
2. *Costs must be identified in detail and laid out on a timeline.*
3. *Fixed costs burden every unit sold until they are covered by sales volume.*
4. *The breakeven point is the number of units which must be sold before the business makes a profit.*

Next lesson: Module 1: Planning, Lesson 5: Defining cash needs

Module 1: Planning
Lesson 5: Defining Cash Needs

Sources of cash, Uses of cash, Example cash forecast, Cash flow projections

In the world of business, cash is king. Cash, however, is not the same as profit. Profit is a good thing, but cash is what makes it possible to keep operating. To operate your business, you will need a cash forecast, and a plan to ensure that you will always have enough. One of the biggest reasons your business may run out of cash is the timing of production of inventory compared to receipt of payment for the product. If your business is growing quickly, you may need to produce more inventory, before you have been paid enough for previous sales to cover the costs of production. In this case, you may be showing profits, but run out of cash in the bank to buy supplies. This is why businesses often set up revolving loans at a local bank. The bank covers the cash shortfalls, and gets paid back in a short time.

Sources of Cash
You get cash from payments for sales of your products. You can also get cash from bank loans, loans from others, investors in your company, sales of assets, memberships or recurring fees, maintenance contracts, licenses that you sell, or lease payments from something you are offering. The first step in defining your cash needs is to lay out your sales forecast for each product line, by month. Using your best judgment and your market research data, set up a spreadsheet with each product identified. Forecast your sales by month, in number of products sold for each line. Enter your expectation of the price for each product, and let the spreadsheet calculate a revenue forecast for each product line. Be careful to consider the timing of when you will receive payment for the product. For example, if you receive an order for product delivery in May, but you do not get paid for the product until June, be sure to place the payment in the month of June. You may decide to forecast a price increase or a price

reduction, depending on your judgment about the impact of competition.

Like this:

Sales	Jan	Feb	Mar	Apr	May	Jun	ETC
Prod Qty	4	10	15	20	25	30	40
Price	$1.10	$1.10	$1.10	$1	$.80	$.80	$.80
Revenue (delayed 30 days)	0	$4.40	$11.00	$16.50	$20.00	$20.00	$24.00

Do this for each product line, and add the sales revenue by month. This is your Revenue Forecast.

Your Sources of Cash should also include the initial "capitalization" of your company; that is, the amount of money you are putting in to fund the business in the beginning.

Uses of Cash

You will also need to carefully lay out the cash your company will need, by month. Do you remember the example of Bob's 5-gallon can of varnish? Bob will have to buy that new can, at a cost of $100, as soon as he finishes making 200 walking sticks. On his "Uses of Cash" line, he will match up his sales forecast with his inventory plan. He will note on the plan when he has to buy supplies in bulk, based on his expectation of sales.

Your "Uses of Cash" forecast should lay out every bill you have to pay, by month. Office rent, salaries, health insurance, supplies, phone bills, advertising, taxes, license fees, travel expenses. Every payment you expect to make should be listed by month on your forecast. After you have identified all your bills to be paid, including when you will pay them, you subtract your uses of cash from your sources of cash, by month. Then you show a running balance of your cumulative cash balance, so you can tell when you will run out of money. Your spreadsheet should look like the example on the Master-of-My-Universe website in Figure 1. You will find it as a downloadable file in Module 1, Lesson 5.

As you see in Figure 1, this company needs to have a credit line that goes up to $76,473 in order to cover its cash needs. It expects to be able to pay back that credit line within 6 months. You can see this on the bottom line, where it says "Net Cumulative Cash." What would most impact this forecast, and cause it to not be able to pay back the loan would be . . . higher than forecasted growth. As long as a company is growing quickly, it is a net *user* of cash, not a net generator of cash. It will continue to need investment or loans to keep growing. It is only when the business matures, and reaches its steady state of sales, that the business becomes cash positive. This is almost always true, no matter what industry. This is an important consideration when you think about your personal goals for the company. If you do not want to be under constant pressure to keep cash in the bank – through getting loans and attracting investors – then maybe you don't want the business to grow too quickly. As you develop your cash forecast, you will be making assumptions for each line item. Be sure you note your assumptions, so that when you revisit this, you can decide if your assumptions need to change. Your cumulative cash balance, at the bottom, tells you how much money is left in the bank. When it goes negative, you know you need to plan to get more cash.

Cash flow projections

The cumulative cash balance tells you when you need to get more money, either through a loan or investment. When you carry your spreadsheet out for three or more years, you can project a "return on investment." That is, whatever cash you put into your business through investment, you need to get that cash back, plus more, so that the business will be worth doing. If your most responsible projections cannot show the business providing an appropriate return on its investment money, then you have answered the question: *is there a pot of gold at the end of this rainbow?* If the answer is no, find a different business to focus your time, money, and energy. Entrepreneurs cannot afford to hold too tightly to an idea that is not making money.

Your cash flow projection is not an accounting record. There are many more complexities to actual accounting. It is, however, a guide for management decision-making. The time you invest in preparing your cash forecast will allow you to see what actions you can take to ensure that your business remains viable. Higher than forecasted growth can put an entrepreneur into the position of needing to take either more investment or more debt. You pay attention, learn from your mistakes, adapt to the market, change your behavior, and try again.

Key points:
1. *Timing is everything. Revolving bank loans smooth out the sales cycle and let an entrepreneur sleep at night.*
2. *Small management decisions regarding the payment of bills and the uses of cash can have large implications for the company's cash position.*
3. *Higher than forecasted sales growth can back a company into an undesirable cash corner.*

Next lesson: Module 1: Planning, Lesson 6: Writing the Business Plan

Module 1: Planning
Lesson 6: Writing the Business Plan

The audience for your business plan, Elements of the business plan, Industry profile, Product description, Market analysis, Distribution plan and market strategy, Operational plan, Cash flow, The presentation

You have done most of the work by now for your business plan. You did market research. You analyzed and defined your product and all its cost elements. In the process of defining those costs, you looked at competitive products and checked the pricing strategies of your competitors. The business plan is just the paper where you write down all these thoughts. In the business plan, you record all the assumptions you made when you analyzed your projected sales and estimated costs.

The audience for your business plan
If you are asking for loans or investment for your business, the audience for your plan is the person who is considering investing in your company or loaning you money. If you expect to self-fund the business, (meaning, pay for it yourself,) you and your management team are the audience. The purpose of the plan will be to guide your management decision making. Even if you are self-funding the business, you need this plan. It helps you focus on the goal, and test the sensitivities of your decisions. You will continually update this plan, as you learn more about your customers.

Elements of the business plan
Your Elevator Pitch is the first section of the business plan. It should be named "Executive Summary." It is actually the two minute sales pitch you make if you are selling someone on investing in your business. You have to be able to pitch your business as if the only time you have to speak is on the elevator, riding to a meeting. You need this elevator pitch, even if you are not looking for investors. Defining your business succinctly is helpful to sell the company to potential customers, management

team members, and bank loan officers, too. Spend time on your elevator pitch. It structures the business and gives it direction. Write this first, and design the rest of your business around it. Succinctly define your business with a clear focus, in this two minute pitch. Then build the rest of your plan around that clear definition.

After the Elevator Pitch, your next section is your Vision Statement. Why is your business meaningful and important to the world? Nobody wants to get involved in something that is unimportant or meaningless. This section can be just a long paragraph. In 150 words or less, describe what is unique, distinctive, and passionate about your dream. Make the reader believe in *you*, the entrepreneur. Make them feel how deeply you care about this business idea. Investors, particularly, understand how much effort will be involved to succeed in your business. They have to know that the entrepreneur cares enough to make it work.

Industry Profile
The next page or two of your plan should describe the industry in which your company will operate. What is the current state of the industry? Is it dominated by major competitors, who have significant branding already in place? Are there just a few competitors, with a stranglehold on the market? If so, you will, later in the plan, need to describe how you will carve out a unique niche to erode their market share. Is the market characterized by many diverse competitors, none of whom have established a dominant position? One mistake many entrepreneurs make is to say there are no competitors, and their product is new and innovative. Their argument is that it will make its own market, and define a new industry. This is one thing experienced investors will look for: *if there are no competitors, there are no customers. If your product is a breakthrough technology, which never before existed, let Apple and Microsoft introduce it.* It is too difficult for a small, new company to teach customers that they want something they have never wanted before. Your potential customers have some

substitute for your product that is currently filling their need. Maybe that substitute is unsatisfactory in many ways. Your intent is to convince them to stop doing what they are doing now, and buy your product instead. But, if customers have a need, they are filling it. You must persuade them that you can fill it better. Your customers do not have a need that is sitting there unresolved. They will only see the value of your product if you can show them it is better, faster, cheaper, or more satisfying than whatever they are doing now. If they are doing nothing now, they do not need your product and will not buy it.

> ***Question:*** *What about Facebook? Nobody needed Facebook before they had it, and then, all of a sudden, millions of people couldn't live without it.*
>
> ***Answer:*** *Before, people used the telephone to do what they do on Facebook. Facebook is allowing them to do more of what they were doing on the telephone. Customers are doing something now, to solve every problem. You have to assess what substitute they are using. If your product is not perceived to be better than what they are doing now, they will not switch.*

Product Description

After you define the industry in which you are working, the next step is to describe your product. You must show how your product is different from, better than, and higher value to the customer than the alternatives available to them. In describing your product, it is not acceptable to just list the features. You must list the benefits to the customer, not just the features of the product.

Market Analysis

You described the industry in which you will work, but now you must go to the next level and describe the customers who will choose your product over the existing products and alternative available to them. Why does this particular type of customer want the benefits that your product offers, over and above any competitive product or alternative solution? After you describe the type of customer who will buy from you, you must go on to identify how many customers there may be who are that type. You must guess at how big the market is, but you must base your guess on as much data as you can find.

Distribution Plan/ Marketing Strategy
Next, after you have defined the target customer and sized the market, you must show that you know how to find that customer, and how to get your product into their hands. How and where is this customer looking for a product like yours? How can you identify specifically who they are and deliver your targeted message to them? Are they members of the same club? Do they shop in the same stores? Do they live in the same geographic area? Do they buy another type of product that is an accessory to yours? Do they read the same magazines? Do they attend the same events? Where will you meet them, with your marketing message? You cannot broadcast your message to everyone in the world, because it is too expensive to do that. How will you identify your potential customers, and tell them about the benefits of your product? If you cannot find your target market, you will waste too many dollars advertising to people who will never buy. Fortunately, Internet marketing has allowed potential customers to self-identify. What words will they search when they surf the Internet? In this section of your business plan, fully describe how you will find your customers to deliver your message. Describe your Internet marketing strategy as a component of your marketing plan.

Operational Plan
The next section of your business plan is your strategy for operations. Do you need to build a factory for mass production of your product? Are you going to license your idea and have others make the physical product? Are you thinking of building a franchise? Are you going to begin by producing a few products in your basement? What is your organizational chart, and how does it change over time? What types of positions will you need, and when will you hire them as you grow? Most importantly,

what is the experience and background of your management team?

Cash Flow

Finally, you will include your cash forecast, and the assumptions you used to make it. The cash forecast defines how much money you need to make this business succeed. It also shows your projections of when the investors will get the return on their money, or when the loan will be repaid. If you are using this business plan to attract investment or loans, you will need your financial projections to be transformed into an actual balance sheet, profit and loss statement, and pro forma projections. You will need an experienced accountant to work that out for you.

The Presentation

After you put your business plan into a nicely formatted document, with a title page, a nice cover, and a little one-page non-disclosure statement for readers to sign, you also need to make a PowerPoint presentation. You are going to be delivering this presentation orally, and answering questions, if you are going to ask for money. If you are not going to ask for money, you will be delivering a version of it to your employees or management team, to rally the troops around the mission. Most entrepreneurs will ask those who get copies of a business plan to sign a statement saying they will not disclose the contents. You would also number each copy of the plan, and note to whom you gave it. You would ask for your plan to be returned after reading.

As the entrepreneur, you are the advocate for this business. To effectively advocate for a startup business, you must be more than positive. You must be evangelistic. That is why, when you select a business, you must, as the famous mythologist Joseph Campbell said, "Follow your bliss."

Key points:
1. *The business plan helps to focus the goals and test sensitivities.*
2. *The elevator pitch succinctly defines your business.*
3. *If you have no competitors, how do you know you have a market?*
4. *The business plan must size the market and describe the target customer.*
5. *The management team is a key component of the business plan.*
6. *The entrepreneur must be the company's evangelist.*

Next lesson: Module 1: Planning EXERCISES
Or
Module 2: Funding. Lesson 1: Sources of Cash

Module 1: Planning

Exercises

1. Think about the business you would like to start. Write down your ideas about how to do it. What products or services will you offer? Who will want to buy them? Describe the type of person who would be interested in your products. What benefits do your products provide for the customer? Why would they buy your product instead of any others?

2. Consider the marketing plan for your products. How would you reach the type of person who might be your customer? Write up a one page description of how you will find your customers and deliver your product to them.

3. Using the Internet, find the competitors for your product. What are the alternative solutions your customers use to substitute for your product now? Write up a description of the competitive environment into which you will sell.

Next lesson: Module 1: Planning QUIZ
Or
Module 2: Funding, Lesson 1: Sources of cash

Join others on the AliceElliottBrown.com Business Blog to discuss your plans.

Module 1: Planning Quiz

1. What is the best way to select a product or service for your business?
    a. Find something that is likely to have a very big market.
    b. Choose something that you like to spend time doing.
    c. Pick something that can be sold at a very low cost.
    d. Choose something that is currently very popular.
2. How can a "niche" market product overcome the lure of the Big Box stores, and sell an expensive product?
    a. By dominating a small, exclusive segment with a unique product offering.
    b. By having a large advertising budget
    c. By giving away discount coupons
    d. By suing Wal-Mart
3. How can you decide your price for your product?
    a. Add up your costs and add a profit
    b. Price your product the same as your competitors
    c. Price your product less than your competitors
    d. Test the value of your product against what customers believe it is worth
4. Which of the following cost elements is a fixed cost?
    a. The labor it takes to make one product
    b. The office rent
    c. Sales tax
    d. Shipping
5. When your cash forecast shows that you will run out of money in 5 months, you should:
    a. Ignore it and hope for the best
    b. Change the assumptions and run the numbers again
    c. Apply for a loan or ask for more investment
    d. Run down inventory and reduce reserves.
6. The purpose of a business plan is:
    a. To put the best spin possible on your company.
    b. To identify corporate weaknesses

c. To attract investors
d. To focus management decision-making.

Find answers to the quiz and get feedback online at
AliceElliottBrown.com

Module 2: Funding

2-1: Sources of cash
2-2: Debt vs equity
2-3: About vulture capital
2-4: The perils of taking money from friends
2-5: Mortgaging your house
2-6: Shoestrings and bootstraps

Module 2: Funding
Lesson 1: Sources of Cash

Use your savings, Run up your credit cards, Mortgage your house, Borrow from your retirement plan, Be cautious about friends and family, Look for an angel, Run on a shoestring, Get supplier credit, Bootstrap your company

Once you have written your business plan, you will have a good "first draft guess" at how much money you need. Your cash forecast defines the timing of the money. Now you need to figure out how to get it. Your first consideration in cash planning is to find a way to 'self-fund.' You want your business to pay for itself as it goes. For example, maybe you don't need to start out in an office.   Maybe you can start by working out of your basement.   After sales come in, you can move to an office, when there is some cash being generated.   You also might start by doing the work yourself, hiring no employees. You might increase the responsibilities of your partners, and take on the marketing tasks yourself. You might trim the advertising budget and focus purely on Internet advertising.   Once you have reviewed your plans, and found ways to do things as effectively as possible, you will have the plan in your hand that requires the least cash.

Use your savings

What money do you have? Whatever you have, plan to put your own money into the business first.   It may sound like a great idea, when textbooks tell you to use "Other People's Money" to start your business. But, think about that. If you were the investor, would you risk your money to invest in a business whose owner was not confident and passionate enough to open his or her own wallet?   If you believe in your business and yourself, and if you have done everything you can to understand your target customer, then "leap and the net will appear." Don't hold back. If you have partners in this business, they, too, must put in their own money. The distribution of the partnership profits is based on the amount invested proportionally by each partner.

Run up your credit cards

Get those teaser introductory rates at 0%, or better yet, get the ones that are 1.99% for the length of the loan. Credit cards are generally not secured by your house, so if the worst happens, and you declare bankruptcy, well, that is sad. Very sad.

Mortgage your house

Don't do this unless you are really sure the business is going to at least be able to keep making the mortgage payments for you. If you do go to a bank to ask for a loan, however, they will most likely tell you to put the house up as collateral. In fact, you can expect that will be the deal for any loan. You will find plenty of textbooks that tell you the Small Business Administration is a prime prospect to give you a loan-guarantee. However, read the SBA website.
http://www.sba.gov/financialassistance/

The website says:

> Documentation requirements may vary; contact your lender for information you must supply. Common requirements include: purpose of the loan, history of the business, financial statements for three years (existing businesses), schedule of term debts (existing businesses), aging of accounts receivable and payable (existing businesses), projected opening-day balance sheet (new businesses), lease details, amount of investment in the business by the owner(s), projections of income, expenses and cash flow, signed personal financial statements and personal resume(s). You should take the information, including your loan proposal and submit it to a local lender. If the lender is unable to approve your loan, you may ask if the lender can consider your request under the SBA loan guaranty program. Under this program, the SBA can guaranty up to 85% of a small business loan; however,

the lender must agree to loaning the money with the SBA guarantee. The lender will then forward your loan application and a credit analysis to the nearest SBA District Office. After receiving all documentation, the SBA analyzes the entire application, then makes its decision.

The SBA primarily gives loan guarantees to ongoing businesses, with provable cash flows over two or three years.   But, risk takers and venture adventurers, they are not. If you are serious about getting a bank loan, expect to pull out the deed for your house.

Borrow from your 401K Plans and Life Insurance Plans
This is a particularly good place to borrow money. If you don't pay it back, you lose the potential future benefit.   A lot can happen in the future, including a complete stock market crash that would have made your 401K plan worthless anyway. If you have one, borrow the money out of it.

Ask Friends and Relatives to be Investors
Venture capitalists provide money to ongoing businesses, seldom real startups. The risk in borrowing money from your friends and relatives is that you will lose them as friends if you can't pay them back.   If, however, you offer a formal investment opportunity, perhaps they will make money if you succeed. Be sure the opportunity is formally documented, and be sure you give them what you promise.   It is better to bring in the creepy brother-in-law and the distant cousin, rather than the close relatives to whom you must turn for support when times get rough.

Look for an "Angel"
Much has been said about these alleged "angel" investors who fund startups. The probability is not zero that your angel may turn out to be a scam artist trying to take you for what little you do have. When people are chasing a dream, they can sometimes be gullible and vulnerable.

Plan to operate on a shoestring

Particularly when you are starting up, run your company efficiently, with no frills. There is nothing more galling to a friend and family investor than to see you using their investment money to pay for unnecessary expenses that seem excessive and frivolous.

Get credit from your suppliers

If your suppliers will give you 90 days to pay, and you are able to produce a product, sell it, and collect the money in 85 days, you are home free. Don't assume that a supplier's formal policies are set in stone. They may tell you they won't wait for their money, but if you talk to them, tell them about yourself and your business, it can sometimes happen. Of course, if you just don't pay your suppliers on time, that means they won't re-supply you until you do. That might be an option. As an entrepreneur, you will make hard decisions objectively, calculating the cost of what you do, not the rightness or wrongness of it.

Bootstrap it

What if you don't have any money and you can't get any? This could happen. It could be a time in your life when you just do not have any money to risk. What if you don't own a house? In that case, you will have to plan your business around a 'self-funding' scenario. Your own consulting services may have to be one of your products. Essentially, your time will have to be the substitute for money. You will have to run everything on a shoestring and a bootstrap, until something can be sold to fund the business. Your business will have to become more service-oriented initially. You may have to keep your day job. If your business is one which you enjoy, then spend your time doing it after work. Get it ready while you still have an income, and figure out the self-funding ways to make it happen.

Key points:
1. *The most likely sources of funds for your business are your savings, your retirement plan, and your credit.*
2. *If you have partners, they also need to provide funding. Ownership in the business is calculated by money invested.*
3. *However much money you raise, you still need to run your business in the most cost-effective way.*
4. *Review your business plan and look for services you can sell to help self-fund your company.*

Next Lesson: Module 2: Funding, Lesson 2: Debt vs Equity

Module 2: Funding
Lesson 2: Debt vs Equity

Other People's Money, Corporate stock, SBA loans, Key financial ratios, Industry standards

Which is better, loans or investments? Investors own an equity piece of your business. How much cash you take in loans (debt) vs how much cash you take in investment (equity), has a large bearing on the kind of business you'll run, and the quality of your life. Loans are extremely stressful. You must make a specific payment on them, on a specific time schedule. Loans do not care whether the economy is good or bad. They do not understand when you miss a payment. If your business has a slow month, you cannot call the lender and offer an explanation. You cannot issue a press release telling vendors you have decided to postpone payment for a while. That is the bad side of debt.

The good side of debt, however, is that you do not lose control of your business; at least, not unless your creditors take you to court and demand a forfeiture of assets. Creditors are not business owners, and they do not have the option to require you to run your business according to their rules. Investors, however, are part owners of your business, and they can give you a lot more trouble than they are worth. Either way, taking Other People's Money to run your business creates stress.

Other People's Money
Investors can be formal institutional investors, like venture capitalists. Until you are bringing in about $4M annually in revenue, you aren't likely to be on their list. More likely, despite your best efforts to avoid taking money from friends and family, your investors will probably be friends and family. If you have investors, you will want to be a formal corporation, with formally issued stock. You can have both voting stock and non-voting stock. If you have friends and family investors, try to sell them non-voting stock. Otherwise, they will be putting their

two cents in when you can't take it. Sadly, you are going to need to pay a lawyer to set this up for you.

Corporate stock

You can issue corporate stock, even if you are not a public company listed on a stock exchange. To do this, you must get an attorney to register your offering in each state where you will sell your securities. Your stock can have rules associated with its transferability to others.

There is quite a balancing act between taking money as loans or taking it as investment from someone other than yourself. While many advisors will tell you to use Other People's Money wherever you can, the tradeoff is measured in stress. Stress is not typically the purpose of running your own business, so this handbook is telling you: try to self-fund whenever you can. If you can't, try to issue non-voting stock first. If that will not raise enough money, third choice is bank debt on your assets. Worst case is high interest debt or dilution of your ownership to the point that you lose control.

SBA loans

As your business builds a history, you may be able to get loans that are guaranteed by the Small Business Administration. These loans are issued by commercial banks. The procedure is to ask for a loan first, get turned down, and then ask the SBA to back the loan.

Key Financial Ratios

While you don't personally have to learn the intricate details of accounting, it is important to understand some "rules of thumb" that describe the financial health of your business.   As a manager, you can learn to read your accountant's reports, and check for these indicators of solid financial management.   You will need to learn to read your balance sheet, and your income statement. Then, you can calculate your company's Quick Ratio, Debt Ratio, Day's Inventory, Day's Sales Outstanding, and Return on Assets Ratio. These are measures of the balance of the elements of your operation. You should use these "rules of thumb" to make management decisions about how you will operate.

Quick Ratio = (Current Assets – Inventory)/Current Liabilities. This ratio is a measure of a company's capacity to repay current debts, if all sales stopped immediately.

Debt Ratio = Total Liabilities/Total Assets. This ratio measures the percent of a firm's assets which are financed by its creditors.

Days' Inventory = (Cost of Goods Sold/Average Inventory)/365 days. This tells you how fast the merchandise is moving through the business. It is a measure of how many times you turn the inventory in a year. Higher number of inventory turns is better.

Days' Sales Outstanding = Days in accounting period/Receivables turnover ratio. To calculate the Receivables turnover ratio, divide the Net Sales by the Accounts Receivable. The Days' Sales Outstanding tells the average number of days it takes to collect the accounts receivable. There is no point in selling something, if you don't get paid for it!

Return on Net Worth = Net Income/Owner's Equity X 100%. This tells you whether or not you are taking the gold out of that pot at the end of the rainbow, and depositing in the bank. It tells you how much you are earning on the money you have invested in the business.

Industry standards

Each of these ratios will have a corresponding standard in your industry. Look up your competitors' 10K reports, if they are public companies, or ask your accountant to tell you a reasonable standard for each ratio for your industry. Then, if you find that your business does not line up with the standards, question your accountant about what management actions you could take to bring financial balance.

Key points:
1. *Debt is stressful, but losing control of your business is worse.*
2. *Using Other People's Money is not all it's cracked up to be.*
3. *You can issue non-voting stock, if you can find someone to buy it.*
4. *SBA-backed loans may become viable as you grow and document a sales history.*
5. *Accounting rules of thumb help you make better management decisions to manage your cash position.*

Next Lesson: Module 2: Funding, Lesson 3: About Vulture Capital

Module 2: Funding
Lesson 3: About Vulture Capital

Who is the fish?, Expand or die, In for the kill, The stages of venture capital, Exit strategy

It sounds so enticing. A venture capital company, coming in with millions in funding. And, management help, too! They're involved with their partners businesses; they're going to help you with your management; they *listen*! They have experienced managers on staff, who have so much to offer you! They can offer "tips" for your business, a shoulder to cry on, and qualified people to be part of your brainstorming! They *enhance* your business and make it better! You need them, because you can't meet the cash needs of your growing customer base, unless they front you $4M. Well, I guess if your business plan says you need $4M to take the next step, then you're going to have to sit down at the table with a venture capitalist. Some businesses do need that, and there is no choice.

Who is the fish?
Except . . . they actually aren't going to give you $4M all at once. They're just going to let it out a little at a time, the way a fisherman lets out the string slowly, waiting for the fish to take the hook. As the fish, why do you care? If you like the bait, and you want the bait, why not eat it?

There really is only one reason. The venture capitalist is going to take your business. Not now, while there is still a lot of work to be done. Now, the business needs you. You are the entrepreneur, with the passion and the vision and the laser-focused dedication. The venture capitalist is not going to take it from you now, while it is an infant and needs to be suckled at your breast, fed every two hours, and monitored day and night. While this business is a baby, it is still going to be yours. In fact, the venture capitalist won't open the wallet until you've got this baby at least potty-trained and toddling. All the hard work and the risk? That's going to be yours to take. The venture capitalist may talk nicely on the telephone, throw you some praise and adulation here and there, and float into town in a private jet to take you out to dinner occasionally. But, while you are nurturing a startup, the Venture Capitalist doesn't invest. He just watches. Like a vulture, waiting for its prey to weaken.

Expand or die

After an exhausting struggle, you succeed in your business. You eventually get to $3M in annual sales. The VC starts talking to you about expansion. He helps you figure out what it would take to grow, so you can really take advantage of the market. You brainstorm with him about the necessity to strike while the iron is hot. He points out that if you do not get a major cash infusion now, you will be left behind, as your market share shrinks, and others take the prize.

He tells you how much he respects you, and what you've done. He points out how useful he's been in your process. He describes what the two of you could do together. He offers you $4M. You sign. He gives you the first $500K. Then, just as your business is cresting, from startup to ongoing concern, just as it is going from a cash eater to a cash generator, just as it is becoming a real business that could offer a decent lifestyle in an attractive small business . . .

In for the kill

He tells you you need another round of financing. The first 500K was not enough, but for the next, you must dilute your ownership again. You watch as your percentage of ownership shrinks. You keep working. With this next set of money, the business is finally on its feet. You've done it. It's working. All your sweat is paying off, and the baby is on its feet, walking on its own. You birthed it, and it's entering the big leagues. The venture capitalist says it's time for "professional" management.

He pulls his trump card and throws you out. That's the pattern. It's what Vulture Capital is. Like it or not. Not right, not wrong, just *true.* Not good, not bad, just *what happens next.*

If you had the foresight to make the right deal in the beginning, you can waltz off into the sunset with a treasure in your bank. But if you didn't negotiate the deal with this in mind, you will be *eaten*.

The stages of venture capital

Venture capital firms invest about seven percent of all funding for private corporations. Some of those firms are owned by corporations, who "spin out" divisions or product lines as new companies. Some are owned by states, who set them up to do economic development for jobs in their blighted areas. Some are owned by the Central Intelligence Agency, who does . . . whatever. More than ninety percent of applications received by venture capital companies will be rejected before screening. They don't meet the basic criteria for consideration.

About one percent of the seven percent of funding from venture capitalists goes to initial stage companies who are startup businesses. Most V.C. money goes to companies which have been operating for more than three years, have proven themselves, and are looking for money for expansion. What makes a deal attractive to a V.C. is the potential for a high return on their investment and an exit strategy to realize that return within three to five years.

Exit strategy

For the V.C., that exit strategy typically is a plan to take the company to an IPO (Initial Public Offering). If this happens, you, as the founding CEO, are most likely out on your ear. Had you known and understood this to be the plan, you would have structured your deal to account for it. You could take your money and retire. Which, of course, you must do, because you signed a "non-compete" agreement when they gave you the investment money. If, however, you went into this deal picturing yourself continuing to run the business, you may not have gotten the terms which lead to a happy ending.

Key points:
1. *Venture capital companies are not typically funding start-up businesses.*
2. *Entrepreneurs who are just looking for an attractive small business to support their families, can safely cross 'look for venture capital' off their To-do lists.*
3. *If you have built a successful small business and are looking to expand it, take it public, cash in, and retire, this might be a path. Unless you can swim, however, you might not want to get into that boat.*

Next Lesson: Module 2: Funding, Lesson 4: The Perils of Taking Money From Friends

Module 2: Funding
Lesson 4: The Perils of Taking Money from Friends and Family

Fall down seven times, Who has seen an angel, Just in case, Selling stock

Where can you get money to start a business? If you are under 30 years old and your parents are rich, there is no problem. Let your parents stake you. But if that is not the case, asking for money from friends and family has a high probability of causing you to damage your relationships with them.

If you've ever sold insurance, Amway, Herbalife, or any of the multi-level marketing products, you know that conventional wisdom tells you to go rope in all your friends and cut them in on this fantastic deal. After all, you believe in it, so why wouldn't you want to let them in on a good thing? There are occasions when that policy works out well. If everyone who listens to your pitch believes the product they've bought is a good product, then fine. All is well. But selling your business to your friends and family is something altogether different. You see, when your business is new, and it has not proven itself to make money, then all you can sell to your friends and family is *yourself.* They will buy into the business because they believe in *you.* They will hand over their money to show their confidence in your capability. What does that mean if your business fails? It means *you* failed. Your friends and family, having invested in *you*, will see *you* as a personal failure. They won't think the business failed, as many businesses do. They will think *you* failed, and they will withdraw their confidence and treat you differently.

Fall down seven times
If you are going to be an entrepreneur, you can't personalize a business failure. You have to follow the Japanese adage: Fall down seven times, get up eight. You have to understand that a business failure is not your personal failure, so that you can keep getting up. Startup businesses do fail, and they fail frequently.

Some studies say eight out of ten new businesses will fail. It can happen to you. You might have to start a new business four times, failing every time, before you do it again and finally hit it right. Practice makes perfect! The problem is, if your best friends and closest family look at you through eyes that call you a failure, it will be hard for you to keep yourself from agreeing with them. It is best not to get those people involved in your business who must remain in place as your personal support system. How can you keep getting up after you've been knocked down, when you have disappointed those you love? You need to keep your self-confidence in place, so that you can keep trying until you get it right. This is why you really don't want money from your best friends.

Who has seen an angel?

So, if you can't take money from your friends or your family, who would take a risk on you? It is said, although it may be an urban legend, that there are mysterious secret benefactors who have money to burn, and are willing to risk it on a promising business plan and an earnest entrepreneur. The stories sound a lot like: *Go to Hollywood and work as a waitress in a diner until you are discovered.* Stranger things have happened.

Just in case

Just in case you happen to meet one of these angels, carry your business plan around with you. Meanwhile, Uncle Joe's second wife's third cousin, who you don't really care if you never see again, has heard that you are an up-and-comer, and wants to get in on the action. You are aware that he is no angel, but you know that losing the money he invests with you will not significantly harm his family. What do you do?

Selling stock

You incorporate your business. You set the classes of stock, making sure Uncle Joe's cousin gets only non-voting stock, Class B. You limit the amount of money you will take from any one investor to an amount that is nominal relative to their assets. You bite the bullet and pay the lawyer for setting this up. You raise the money from people who want to get in on the ground floor of a good thing. You sell your stock to people who think they are playing the lottery. This is fine. Just be absolutely certain the people who play can afford the game.

Key points:
1. *Small businesses fail. You cannot take this failure personally, but if you have lost the money of your friends and family, they will take it out on you. You cannot afford that, at any price.*
2. *It is said that there are "angel" investors who invest in small businesses. Good luck finding one.*
3. *You can sell stock in your company directly. There are rules to follow if you do this. Be sure to follow them carefully and diligently. There is always a market for the next big thing.*

Next lesson: Module 2: Funding, Lesson 5: Mortgaging your house

Module 2: Funding
Lesson 5: Mortgaging your house

Leap and the net will appear, Are you crazy?, Tuna fish and homelessness

When the rubber hits the road, your small business is most likely going to be funded by the equity in your house. *Probably.* Yes, you can go to the Small Business Administration and try to get a loan guarantee for bank funding. But, *probably*, it won't work. The SBA guarantees loans, but *most likely*, that's after you've gotten things rolling on your own and you've got more than a million dollars in annual sales.   If you read the information posted on the SBA website, you might get the impression that you can get the SBA to guarantee a bank loan to start your business. Sometimes, there are conferences and seminars which actually say this. Who knows? Maybe it has happened. Maybe it will happen to you. But, *probably*, it won't. So, as a responsible and serious entrepreneur, when you are writing your business plan . . . don't count on it.

http://sba.gov/mostrequesteditems/CON_FAQ1.html

Leap and the net will appear
If you've got a house with equity, plan to take loans out against it. However, in your application for those loans, you will have to be able to prove you can pay the monthly payments. This means: don't quit your job, because the bank will not accept your business plan as a valid guarantee of a salary for you. It's a dilemma.

Here are the ways you can get money to start your business:
1.   Use your savings, including your 401K and your life insurance policies.
2.   Use the savings of every person you are going to bring into your management team and make a founder of the business.

3. Run up your unsecured credit cards to their maximum limits.
4. Come up with a scheme to get paid by your customers before you have to pay your suppliers.
5. Mortgage your house.

In other words, risk everything. Leap, so the net will appear.

The rest of the ways you will read about in conventional textbooks? Sell stock to your friends and family, borrow money from the SBA, and submit your business plan to venture capitalists? *Probably not. You can give it a try. But in the end, it **probably** won't work.*

Are you crazy?

If this scheme of risking everything sounds crazy, don't do it. The average new business startup can be done for less than $15,000. If your business plan requires a six-figure investment, change your plan. Make a plan to start smaller, and fund your company with sales of services. If your business idea is the next Facebook, Amazon, Google, or eBay, you may not be able to go it alone without investors. In that case, keep your assets safe and keep shopping for those angels. But, if your business plan is designed to be the standard, run-of-the-mill, attractive small business, which supports your family and pays your bills, then look yourself in the eye and decide whether you are a CEO or a nutcase. Do what you have to do.

Tuna fish and homelessness

If you don't own a house, you live paycheck to paycheck, and you have no savings, what can you do? If you've already ruined your credit rating trying another business, and you already eat tuna fish for three days before payday, can you still start a business?

Of course. Your plan has to be self-funding.

Key points:
1. *The probability is that you will not get outside investment.*
2. *You will have to make the decision about how much to risk. Decision-making is what entrepreneurs do.*
3. *The average new business can be started for less than $15K.*
4. *Rewrite your business plan until it self-funds.*

Next lesson: Module 2: Funding, Lesson 6: Shoestrings and Bootstraps

Module 2: Funding
Lesson 6: Shoestrings and Bootstraps

Big Cheeses need not apply, Squeeze those nickels, Offer services, Delay payments, Collect quickly, Differentiate your offering, Measure your marketing efforts, Use online marketing and social media, Watch your cash flow

No matter how much money you have raised to start your business, it won't be enough.   Regardless of how well-funded you think you are, you must plan to do things in ways that conserve cash.   For example, some new businesses, thinking they have unlimited funding because they are spinoffs from large corporations, start out with original artwork on the walls, private offices for all managers, and travel budgets for non-essential trips. Wasteful behavior, when exhibited by a startup, insults the investors.

"Big Cheeses" need not apply

A "hired entrepreneur," installed into a new business by his friends in venture capital, believed he was competent. It was his opinion that it was okay to spend $100Million to get this new company running. He hired an interior designer for the glass-walled new offices.   He purchased perfectly working small businesses and broke them like recalcitrant colts.   After five years of investment, the company had a revenue stream of $4M annually.   When the investors pulled the plug, the hired gun left with his buyout and sailed around the world.   Forty employees, however, hit the unemployment office.   They weren't the big spenders who prevented the company from succeeding. They came to work and did their jobs. It was the Hired-Gun-Big-Cheese who cheated the investors and betrayed the employees.

You can't hire an entrepreneur.   They are not for sale.   When you do find one, or if you are one, you will observe that the entrepreneur is keenly aware of how much money is spent on everything.

Squeeze those nickels

In your startup business, if something can be done more efficiently, it should be done so. If a market can be tested before serious money is spent, test it. If you can get suppliers to give you better terms, get them. If you can arrange for customers to pay you faster, arrange it. If you can hold off on buying anything, hold off. Every move you make must be taken with an awareness of how much each thing costs. You can operate your business on a shoestring, and pull yourself up by your bootstraps, as long as you are paying careful attention. By watching your pennies, the dollars take care of themselves.

Offer services as part of the package

One way to self-fund a business is to offer a product mix which includes labor as a component. It takes much less money to sell labor-hours than it does to build a product inventory. By offering a service as part of your product offering, you are able to bring in cash to use to fund your inventory. Your product mix should address the same target customers. That way, your marketing dollars can address the same people's needs. This is called a "focus strategy."

For example, suppose you are building a business to sell organic, non-toxic cleaning products based on a proprietary formula. Your mission may be to grow the products business. While you are getting started, however, you might also offer a cleaning service for business offices. In all your advertising and marketing, you focus on the "green" aspects of your product. Then you tell business owners this form of non-toxic cleaning allows them to advertise themselves as environmentally responsible. When you get cleaning contracts, you hire people for that specific task. You have them do the job with your products. You make money from the cleaning contracts without costs of inventory. Laying it out on your cash forecast, you can see that the cleaning contracts are "cash-positive" jobs.

A strategy for funding your business is to focus on a type of customer, and offer a product line mix which includes both service and product offerings, but which shares advertising and marketing costs.

Delay payment to your suppliers

Transfer balances on your credit cards to new credit cards, if you have to. Time is money. The longer you delay payments, the more opportunity you have to catch up your sales income with your expenses outgo. Don't, however, pay usurious interest rates. Find other ways, and skip debt altogether if you are going to be a victim of the temple moneychangers. In the beginning, you may find your suppliers telling you that they want payment within 30 days. Try to talk to their company president. Try threatening to change suppliers. Take your business elsewhere, if you must. Maybe you will find another hungry entrepreneur who wants to be your supplier, and will agree to 120 days for payment. Pay late, even if they don't agree. Worst case, integrate vertically. That is, make your own supplies from raw materials.

Collect quickly from your customers

While working to get your suppliers to accept payments late, you need your customers to pay early. Collect deposits. Get payment upon delivery. Accept credit cards. Do not agree to trials or consignments. Be certain you are pricing your products correctly, so that you are making money on every sale.

Differentiate your offering

Make your product unique, special, and exclusive, so that you can command a higher price from your target customers. As a small business, you are not in a position to be the low cost producer. Do not compete with the big box stores. People will pay more for products which they perceive to be of higher value, so create that perception of value and deliver it.

Measure your marketing efforts

It can be easy to spend money on marketing and get no results. Do not spend money marketing unless you have measurement systems in place to assess whether the money is well-spent. What good is it to place an ad in a travel brochure, if few people who read that brochure ever come to your town? Why participate in the Chamber of Commerce give-aways if only other Chamber of Commerce members get the prizes? Many times, local retailers get together for joint marketing activities, which end up marketing only to other retailers. You have to know who your customers are, and where they gather. You must "intercept" them during their normal activities, and present them with the information they need to decide to buy, at the time they are thinking of buying. Internet marketing has all the characteristics you need: it meets people where they are looking, and offers them information at the time they want to buy.

Use online marketing and social media

The Internet revolution occurred for good reason. The printing and distribution of information and marketing materials is too expensive to be useful. The Internet equalized the small business and the large business. It was cheap and easy to build a website. Small companies could have websites that were just as fancy and impressive as large companies. Customers could no longer tell the difference! A small company with a great website can make a lot of progress in reaching its customers. The small company that bootstraps it uses the free resources of the Internet to put itself directly in the path of surfing customers. Your path to sales is to give target customers the information they need, at precisely the moment they want to buy.

Be watchful of your cash flow timing

You can bootstrap your business. The key is to watch your cash like a hawk checking for rabbits. Pay carefully. Collect relentlessly. Sell something. Find something somebody wants to buy. Get your product together. Deliver it to somebody who wants to pay for it.

> *Do it again.*
> *Do it again.*
> *Do it again.*

And if you keep on doing it, you will eventually see that there is money in the bank for you to live on.

Key points:
1. *There is never enough money, so make do and count pennies.*
2. *Focus your efforts on cash-positive jobs.*
3. *Pay late, collect early.*
4. *Price high and differentiate your offering.*
5. *Use your online presence.*
6. *Sell something. Keep doing it.*

Next lesson: Module 2: Funding EXERCISES
OR
Module 3: Structuring, Lesson 1: Choosing a Legal Structure

Module 2: Funding EXERCISES

1. Analyze how much money you really need to start your business. Put together a cash plan. Try to find a way to minimize the cash needs for startup.

2. Using the Internet, research your competitors' financial statements. See if you can find their annual reports. What can you learn from their annual reports about the type of company you will be running?

3. Research the standard practices in your industry. Who would be your suppliers? What are their policies for minimum orders? What are their requirements for credit?

Join others to discuss your answers at the AliceElliottBrown.com Business Blog

Module 2: Funding QUIZ

1. The best source of funding for your new business is
    a. The Small Business Administration
    b. Venture Capital
    c. Friends and Family
    d. Loans on your personal assets
2. The Days' Inventory ratio tells you
    a. How fast merchandise is moving
    b. What your competitors are doing
    c. The amount of inventory you have
    d. When to reorder supplies
3. Venture capital companies look for
    a. An opportunity to reap the rewards of someone else's risk and effort
    b. High potential business plans
    c. A solid management team in a startup
    d. Reasonable risk
4. You should ask your friends and family to invest in your business when
    a. You have nowhere else to turn.
    b. Pigs fly
    c. You want to help them get in on the ground floor of an opportunity
    d. You are sure you will succeed.
5. When all else fails, fund your business by
    a. Selling your services and labor
    b. Mortgaging your house
    c. Borrowing from your life insurance
    d. All of the above
6. A startup business should be sure to have
    a. Nice offices, so that customers perceive success
    b. Expense accounts for executives to take customers out to lunch
    c. A booth at the best trade shows
    d. A keen awareness of cash flow

Check your answers at AliceElliottBrown.com

Module 3: Structuring

3-1: Choosing a legal structure
3-2: Filing with the government
3-3: Branding your company
3-4: Hiring yourself and others
3-5: Setting up your website
3.6: Establishing your accounting system

Module 3: Structuring
Lesson 1: Choosing a Legal Structure

Sole proprietor, Partnership, Limited partnership, Corporation, Limited liability corporation, "S" Corporation

There are three basic forms of business structure: sole proprietor, partnership, or corporation. When you start your business, you choose which of those you will be. Here are the reasons why you would choose each one.

Sole proprietor

This is the simplest structure, and almost seventy percent of new businesses choose this form. To start this business, check the licensing laws of your local county. Then, select a business name that is available in your state. Each state usually prints a guide to their laws, and you can get these at your local county administration building. It is also likely they will be on the website for your state or county. Search on the Internet for your state and county plus the words: business license.

> Here is an example from Fairfax County, Virginia.
> http://www.fairfaxcountyeda.org/licenses-and-permits
> In this example, the county has posted a chart telling you which types of businesses need which types of licenses. It also gives phone numbers and contact information to get the right forms. It also tells you where to call to register the name of your business, and where to check to see if that name is already taken in your state.

You will also need a federal Employer Identification Number (EIN). This is used to open a bank account in the name of your business. Alternatively, you can open a bank account in your own name, and use your social security number as the identifier on the bank account. The EIN is required if you are going to have any employees other than yourself and your spouse.

You can get an EIN instantly online at:

http://www.irs.gov/businesses/small/article/0,,id=102767,00.
html?portlet=4

The sole proprietorship is a business form which has one and only one boss. All decisions are yours. You don't have to sit down to discuss them with any committees. Your signature is on the checks and your bank account gets all the profits. The key consideration for this business form is: the income is reported on your personal 1040 tax form at the end of the year. It is part of Schedule C. If you have another income, from another job, or a spouse's income, and you also run this business, this could be good or bad. If your other income plus this business income gets added together, it could put you in a higher tax bracket It could cause you to lose your ability to take personal deductions. On the other hand, if the business loses money, that loss can reduce the tax on your other income, thus making the net loss lower after tax. Thinking about the tax implications can make your head twirl backwards on your neck like that girl in the Exorcist movie. There can be big advantages to being able to write off your investment in business equipment directly from your personal income tax. The tax savings can be a source of funds for your business.

The simplest business is one in which you are a sole proprietor. Nobody else is involved. The downside to being a sole proprietor is that, if somebody sues the business, they sue *you*. The other downside is that you can't offer an ownership position to key employees, as an incentive to get them to work for a lower salary.

To start this business, call the phone number your state gives you to check on the availability of a business name. Print some business cards on your home computer, open a bank account in the business name, and start telling people you're in business. Shortly thereafter, file the paperwork with your county to get a business license. You will then receive coupons in the mail so you can deposit your sales and payroll taxes, plus instructions for filing electronically. If this is your first time ever being in business for yourself, it is most likely you will choose the sole proprietorship.

Partnerships

When two or more people form a business together, they may decide to choose the "partnership" business structure. Partners get to share in the profits of the firm. Many law firms and consulting companies choose this form. That's why TV shows always have young lawyers dreaming of "making partner." Those profits (or losses) are reported directly on the personal income taxes of each partner. The profits are distributed among the partners according to a formula which is determined by the partners themselves. Often this distribution is determined in a written partnership agreement. Sometimes this agreement is written on the back of a napkin over a beer. The rules about how the partnership will make decisions are entirely up to the partners themselves. Forming a partnership is nearly as easy as a sole proprietorship, as far as government forms are concerned. The hard part is maintaining the relationship with your partners, so that no one takes a free ride from the others. Partners receive a Form K-1, which they report on Schedule E on their income tax. Like the sole proprietorship, there could be a tax advantage if there are business losses, because the losses mean each partner recovers some money from their personal taxes.

> *For example, suppose each of three partners contributes her own used laptop to the business, which she will then use herself for purposes of this business. The used value of each laptop is $800. The business now has an investment of 3 times $800, or $2,400. It carries this investment as an asset on its balance sheet. The partnership also decides to "write this asset off," using the Section 179 depreciation deduction, when it is time to prepare taxes. Now let's say the business had no sales and no other expenses, hypothetically. The business would then have a loss, as*

shown on the income statement, of $2,400. Of course, although it has a loss, it still has the computers, and each partner still uses them. But, the taxes pass through to the partners personal income taxes, so each partner gets to show a loss of $800. This loss reduces each partners income tax payment. Depending on how much other income each partner makes through other sources, this could result in a tax savings per person of up to $300.

Each partner now pays $300 less in income taxes than they would have paid if they had not contributed their computers to the business. The partners can then agree, if they so choose, to each contribute $300 to the business as an investment. This allows the business to get a $900 investment, in real cash. When considering your business structuring, "tax structure" is a potential source of funding. Your accountant should be able to help you identify opportunities, so remember that fact when you choose an accountant. Personal computer software packages are not sufficient for your business needs.

Partnerships, oddly enough, can sometimes be formed after the fact. That is, if you form a partnership before April 15, it can be considered to have been in existence during the transactions of the previous year. This is a description of a *general partnership*. A *limited partnership* is a little bit different.

Limited partnerships
You are probably not going to choose a limited partnership for your new business. A limited partnership is chosen when the business needs to have investors but the founder of the business doesn't want those investors to have any decision making power. General partners are joint owners and must agree on how the business decisions will be made. Limited partners put their money in and passively wait to see whether they get a return on their investment. They also might get a loss which can be declared on their income taxes for a while, waiting for the return. Remember, a loss on your income taxes means less income taxes, provided you have other income. So a limited

partner might possibly sign up, invest, and happily declare losses until such time as the business succeeds and his ship comes in.

Corporations

The third form of structure is the corporation.   These are regulated by states, so you must go to the website for your state, find the instructions to incorporate, and download the forms to register a corporation. If you are going to pay someone to do this for you, let it be your own lawyer. Otherwise, just download the form and do it yourself. In most cases, you are just registering your name and address and declaring your intention. The corporation, unlike the partnership and the sole proprietorship, is its own legal entity. It files its own taxes. Unless you elect to be a special type of corporation called an "S" corporation, the business income does not flow through onto your tax forms.

There are a number of advantages to setting up your company as a corporation. First, if somebody sues the business, they sue the legal entity of the corporation, not you as an individual. Secondly, a corporation offers an opportunity for many people to be "owners." You can issue shares of ownership, which can be used to motivate your management team and employees, and to attract investors.   If you cannot offer some sharing of the potential profits of the business, it is hard to get talented and motivated team members to work with you during the challenging tasks of a business startup.   Many people wonder how a privately-held company can issue shares.   Your startup company will not be listed on any stock exchange, so your shares will not be traded on an open market.   Your shares will just be symbols of the dream.   They will be worth what you can convince others they are worth.   They will have little or no tangible value . . .but if you sell your dream, others may buy it. Others may also dream it, and this will cause them to offer to invest in you.   They invest in you by buying shares in your company, and receiving a stock certificate. Where do you get the stock certificates? You print them off your computer. They are documentation that the person has "bought" a percentage of ownership in your company. You and the investor hope that someday they will have real value.

The normal corporation is called a "C" corporation. On its books, you can be paid as an employee. If you are paid as an employee, then you and the corporation both pay social security and medicare. You also withhold state and federal income tax. You have the option to set up benefits plans for your employees. You can set up retirement plans, health insurance, and other forms of benefits for any employee, including yourself. Benefits plans have many rules attached, and you must use a good accountant to help you do that correctly.

Another reason you need an accountant for a corporation is the "double taxation" of corporate profit. Suppose you actually make money at this business. The corporation shows a profit, and because the corporation itself is a legal entity, that profit is subject to income tax. This tax is declared when the corporation files its tax forms. Then, what happens to the after-tax profits? If you, as the owner, want them, you can declare a "dividend." That is, you can divide them up among all the shareholders and distribute them. You do not have to distribute all the profit. You can just pick whatever portion of the profit you choose to distribute, and reinvest the remainder in the corporation. You must distribute the dividend based on the number of shares each investor owns.

But, how many shares do *you* own? What if you were the person with the idea, and you are the person who does all the work, and you are the person who makes all the decisions, but you didn't have any money to invest in the beginning? How do you get to keep control of your company? This is a very tricky subject. The answer is: you select the rules of your stocks (also called shares) so that the first round that is issued to you cannot be "diluted." You make sure you have 51% of all shares on that first round of stock issuance. You pick a number, out of thin air, and declare that it corresponds to the amount of investment which you personally have invested in the business. For example, suppose you invested $1,000.   You declare that you bought stock at one penny a share, and therefore you own 100,000 shares. You print yourself a stock certificate that says you own 100,000 shares.   There are accounting rules and forms that go along with this, and you get your accountant and your lawyer to do them. Then, when you are ready to take investors into your company, you change the rules about the new shares. The old shares followed Rulebook A. The new shares are a new class and follow Rulebook B. You are the only person who owns shares from Rulebook A.   Maybe you decided that all the shares from Rulebook A cost one penny per share.   However, after you bought your shares, you decided that the business was now far more valuable, because it had obtained your services as a CEO. So all shares purchased after you bought yours were Rulebook B shares.   They cost $5 each.   Your penny shares now are eligible to receive the same dividend per share as each of the $5 shares.

How do you know what goes in the Rulebooks? Surprisingly, you have the right to make your own rules.   It's your business. There are some rules about the rules, however, which cover voting rights and tax treatments, so you will need a good lawyer in addition to a good accountant.

Now, when you distribute profits of the business to yourself, based on your number of shares and the amount of the "dividend," what happens? That money becomes income on your personal 1040 tax return.   But . . . wait. The profits were already taxed, through the corporation's filing. Then you took after-tax profits and gave them to yourself and . . . they got taxed again, when you filed your personal taxes!

If you were the only owner of this corporation, and no other people had invested any money in it or owned any shares, then the solution would be: don't have any corporate profit. Pay out all the money to yourself in salary.   You could be the only owner of a corporation, particularly when it is just starting out. During that time period, that is what you would do. Pay yourself a salary big enough to avoid a corporate profit.   As you get investors, however, your investors will want to see the corporation showing a profit. They will want their share of that profit. That is why you will need a Board of Directors and a team which shares decision-making.

Until you need:
  a) other investors beside yourself,
  b) a W-2 salary so you can apply for a personal loan,
  c) ownership incentives so you can attract a management team without paying them too much, or
  d) protection from personal liability related to your business,

  you can get by with a sole proprietorship instead of a corporation.

Limited Liability Corporations
Partly to reconcile the natural tension between investors and double taxation on dividends, and partly to reduce the overhead of burdensome paperwork, the IRS came up with another form of business structure. The Limited Liability Corporation requires less paperwork than the corporation, and it offers the option to be treated either as a corporation, with its own tax filing, or as a partnership, with the ability to flow through to the partners' personal taxes. It offers less flexibility in issuing direct stock.

"S" Corporations
If you want your corporate income to flow through to your personal taxes, you may select the option, at tax filing time, to declare it to be a Subchapter S Corporation. If you have multiple investors, this could become a very complicated structure. Additionally, Subchapter S corporations are limited on the number of classes of stock they may have (i.e. Rulebook A and Rulebook B become restricted.)

Key points:

1) *The type of structure you choose for your business impacts the tax treatment and the relationship with investors.*
2) *A good accountant is worth the money.*
3) *Until your business is making money, it is really just a hobby. You can safely do your planning and research before filing your business licenses. You will want to keep records of the money you spend doing this, to turn over to your accountant.*
4) *Sole proprietorships, partnerships, Limited Liability Corporations, and S Corporations share the characteristic that their profits or losses can flow directly to the income tax returns of their owners.*
5) *Choose the classic C corporation if you need to have investors to get the business started, if you need stock incentives to give to your management team, or if you want to install a robust employee benefits plan.*

Next lesson: Module 3: Structuring, Lesson 2: Filing with the Government

Module 3: Structuring
Lesson 2: Filing with the government

Business licenses, Payroll taxes, Sales taxes, Personal property taxes, Recordkeeping, Electronic filing

It may seem hard to believe, but the Internal Revenue Service is here to help you.   Regulations for your small business are described, in plain English, on the IRS website. Although you will rely on an accountant to file your paperwork, as the Chief Executive Officer, it is your responsibility to have a basic understanding of the rules of the IRS.   By the time you read the information posted on the IRS website, you will have an excellent grasp of what is involved in running your business, as far as regulations and requirements of the government are concerned.   You can actually watch a video of the IRS tax lessons. http://www.tax.gov/virtualworkshop/
It is very much worth watching.

Business licenses
This link will take you to a list of state websites which will explain regulations for your state.
http://www.irs.gov/businesses/small/article/0,,id=99021,00.html

Setting aside a few days of your time to learn the regulations for doing business in your locality, is an important task for a new CEO.   You won't memorize and understand all of them. However, putting some time upfront into learning basic concepts will allow you to more intelligently hire and manage someone whose energies can be focused on your accounting practices. Initially, this is likely to be an accounting service for which you pay a monthly fee. *It's important.   The CEO should know.* However, the CEO should not be the paperwork keeper and the forms filer.

Spend the day outdoors with the printed versions of the following .pdf files.   Read slowly; take a few notes. By dinner time, you will be nearly an expert on how to keep your small business aligned with government regulations.

The IRS files are updated and maintained at the site:
http://www.irs.gov/businesses/index.html?navmenu=menu1

Payroll taxes
The first file you should print and place in your "IRS" binder is **Publication 15, Circular E, Employer's Tax** Guide. http://www.irs.gov/pub/irs-pdf/p15.pdf

This will explain the basics of payroll taxes and submissions. The gist of it is: you have a chart, and it tells you how much federal income tax to withhold from an employee's check, based on their number of deductions. You know their number of deductions because you asked them to fill out a W-4 form when you hired them. You also have to get the state chart for your state and withhold the state income tax.

There is a formula for how much social security and medicare tax you withhold. You actually withhold half of that from the employee's check, and you pay the other half out of the business. You then have to submit this money on a schedule to the IRS and to your state. It isn't hard, but it's tedious and annoying, so you will want to hire a payroll service to do this, or assign an employee to the task. Of all the forms and schedules and calculations related to your business and the IRS, payroll tax is the one you do not want to screw up.

Sales tax
Sales tax is a state tax, not a federal tax. When you register your business with the state, they will send you coupons to mail in with calculations and money. If you are selling on the Internet, there are special rules. This is something you need to look into for your specific business.

Personal property tax
Some local counties or cities assess a property tax on the

business' assets. This is something you will want to understand before you buy equipment. It may be prudent to lease equipment instead of buying. It depends on the rate of the locality's property tax. You learn about this at your local county office. Find out before you file your first business tax returns.

Recordkeeping

Print **Publication 583: Starting a Business and Keeping Records.** http://www.irs.gov/pub/irs-pdf/p583.pdf
This will explain what you need to have in your files in case of an audit. You can also find extensive explanations of the advantages and disadvantages of each of the forms of business structures: sole proprietorship, partnership, and corporation at:
www.irs.gov/businesses/small/article/0,,id=98359,00.html

This page will also lead you to explanations of the regulations you need to follow. You can apply for an Employer Identification Number online at:
http://www.irs.gov/businesses/small/article/0,,id=102767,00.html

You can get this EIN instantly, and open an online bank account within minutes, using this identification for your business.
After you have spent a day or two becoming familiar with the IRS regulations for business, you will also need to know the rules for your state.

Key points:
> *Payroll taxes are well monitored by the IRS. Do them correctly and diligently.*
> *Record keeping has a lot in common with dental work. Keep up with it routinely, to avoid a disaster that detracts from your ability to continue productive work.*
> *Learn your local laws. Running afoul of the county planning commission will not be worth the aggravation.*

Next lesson: Module 3: Structuring, Lesson 3: Branding your company

Module 3: Structuring
Lesson 3: Branding your company

Competing for mindshare, Pick your theme: make your impression, Communicate your message, A word of caution about customers, Monitor your web presence

An essential, possibly the most essential, factor in selling your products and services is the customer's picture of your company. This image is called your "brand." We all know what a brand is. When we name certain companies, an image comes to mind. Nike. When you hear the word "Nike," you think, "Just do it." You know Nike means athletic shoes. Not sneakers, either. Real, serious, expensive athletic shoes, for the person who means business when they work out. This allows Nike to charge you high prices. You let them do it, because they convince you that you are a better person if you pay more for your sneakers.

> *Kelloggs. You think: "breakfast cereal." You don't want Kelloggs hot sauce.*
>
> *Quaker. You think: "oatmeal." You can't picture Quaker soup.*
>
> *Heinz. You think: "ketchup." Because you are thinking "ketchup," it would be very difficult for you to choose to buy Heinz cheesecake. Your mind automatically pictures the cheesecake with ketchup on it.*
>
> *Smuckers. You think "jelly." Your mind will have trouble choosing to buy Smuckers ketchup. Smuckers is branded as "jelly," so your mind pictures Smuckers ketchup as fruit-flavored.*

Competing for "mindshare"
A company captures an image in your mind of their primary product. Kleenex is a tissue. Kleenex captured so much of your mindshare thinking "tissues," that you call tissues Kleenex, even

when the tissues you are using are not made by the Kleenex company. Because Kleenex has branded itself as tissues, you will have a hard time choosing to buy Kleenex bathing suits. Your mind is associating Kleenex with tissues, and this is done at the subliminal imagery level. The only way Kleenex can sell bathing suits is to change its company name. Otherwise, every potential customer will look at a Kleenex bathing suit on the rack, and get this vision of the bathing suit falling apart like a tissue in the water. If that happens, no one will buy the bathing suits, regardless of their quality and attractiveness.

Your mission as a small business CEO is to get customers to associate your company name with your primary product. That is the purpose of your advertising, the key to your marketing, and the goal of your sales effort. When your company name becomes indelibly written into customers' minds, then they will seek out your product when it is time for them to buy. They will select your product over a competitive product, because your product will be perceived to be the genuine product. Others will be perceived as imitations. They will pay you more for the same thing that others offer, because they will attribute a perceived value to your "brand."

Pick your theme: make your impression
It sounds good. How is it done? To start, you come up with a nice theme for your company. You pick a color scheme for your logo, your ads, your website, and your business cards. You pick a slogan. You pick a font for your company name, which you use on signs, flyers, ads, business cards, and websites. You might even pick a song. Something catchy, like: "I wish I were an Oscar Meyer weiner." Rhyming, sing-song words stick in the head. People's brains associate colors, sounds, and images. You will want to select a set of colors, sounds, and images that will make potential customers automatically think of your company. You pick a company name.

Your company name is critically important. It needs to be memorable. It needs to roll off the tongue. It needs to be four syllables or less. It needs to be translatable in global languages. It does *not* need to be an acronym of letters, unless you only want to sell to the defense department.

You name your products. You write marketing material that talks about how the customer is changed by your product. An important consideration? Scent is the most memorable aspect of human senses. Your product needs to smell good. The scent that occurs when your product is used will act like a retrieval index for the memory of your product. If there is a smell, be sure it is a pleasant one.

> *Tip: In your marketing materials, say: "Using BadaBoom makeup causes me to feel healthy and beautiful." Not: "BadaBoom makeup is made from healthy ingredients."*
>
> *Say: "JeepersCreepers prescription eyeglasses make me look sultry and seductive." Not: "JeepersCreepers glasses are precision-ground from fine sand."*
>
> *Say: "Just do it." Not: "Nike athletic shoes are precision-engineered and hand-sown."*
>
> *Say: "He loves my smile." Not: "BrightWhite toothpaste tears the enamel off your teeth so they look whiter."*

Even product names carry a subliminal meaning. It would be a perfect world if "made in America" held enough sway to cause you to get a higher price for your product. Until the world achieves perfection, however, your only means of getting a higher price is to give the impression that your product is exclusive, unique, and special. You can give that impression in your marketing message by associating the product with improvements in the person who buys it.

Communicating your message
After you come up with your consistent, themed, and visual message, you need to get the word out. Only a few years ago,

getting the word out meant spending a lot of money on media. You needed ads in newspapers, magazines, radio, and television. Flyers to post in grocery stores cost significant money for making copies. Ads and printed media are expensive. Internet websites, Facebook pages, Twitter posts, and Blogs, however, are not expensive. Unless you are starting your business with entirely too much money, you are going to create your brand using the "social media" available on the Internet. This is easier said than done, but it's cheap. You will create your branding through the use of informational website content, social commentary, group interaction, and the instigation of an excited "buzz" on the Internet. It's going to take you, personally, as the CEO, to create that excitement. You are the chief evangelist of your company. Your time will best be spent stirring up the crowd. Once you've got the buzz going, you will have your "brand."

A word of caution about customers

Once you get people talking about your product on the Internet, you lose the ability to control what they say. People are more motivated to post about a product or company that annoyed them than they are to post praise. You have to work to get them to post praise. This will help to nullify the ones who post negative comments. You can get people talking, but nothing will make your product sell unless customers actually want what you are selling. If you've got a product which is a solution looking for a problem, all the Internet marketing in the Milky Way will not sell it. Buzz only sells stuff worth buzzing about.

Monitor your web presence

Buzz on the Internet is the great equalizer of business today. Both small and large companies have an equal opportunity to get customer access through online search engines. More importantly, customer behavior has embraced the practice of using the Internet to research purchases. Consumers now make it a habit to investigate online before they buy. Consumers compare products and prices online. Your product must come up on the first page in relevant searches. It must present favorably in comparison to its alternatives. More importantly, your product must deliver what its marketing message promises. If your product does not deliver, people will know. People will talk about it online and describe their experiences. *It's just what they do.* You can't control the conversation, but you need to participate in it and state your case.

Key points:
1) *Your "brand" is the association which the consumers make about you in their mind.*
2) *Sounds, images, colors, and rhymes write these associations into people's memories. The associations are recalled when purchase decisions are made.*
3) *You must sell how the product enhances the person, not how good the product is.*
4) *People research their product choices on the Internet.*
5) *Your presence on the Internet influences your sales.*
6) *For long term success, your product must deliver what your marketing message sells.*

Next lesson: Module 3: Structuring, Lesson 4: Hiring yourself and others

Module 3: Structuring
Lesson 4: Hiring yourself and others

The business structure determines how you get paid, Applying for credit, Making social security payments, Paying consultants

When you start a business, you are working for it. You need to get paid. The people you hire need to get paid, too. *Don't just take the money out of the cash drawer.* The right way to pay yourself and your employees is to have each employee fill out a Form W-4 from the IRS, so that you can figure out how much to withhold for payroll tax. If you are a sole proprietor, with no employees, you do not have to withhold payroll tax from your checks. Instead, you will have to pay estimated tax personally each quarter, guessing how much you will make at the end of the year, and making sure you pay tax on it in equal installments before it happens. *In a startup business with little history, this borders on the ludicrous.* You don't know enough to guess correctly, so you will either overpay or incur penalties for underpayment. This is just one more example of how much better it would be, from a tax standpoint, to structure yourself as a corporation instead of a sole proprietorship.

The business structure determines how you get paid

For the sole proprietor and the partnership, your payment is made directly from the profits of the company. You will have to estimate your income, and make *equal* tax payments, quarterly, throughout the year. The downside to that system, of course, is that you are not going to be a very good estimator of how much you are going to make from the business, in the beginning. Paying you is the last priority for this business. Whatever goes wrong, taking away *your* money (which is profit) is the first action. If you wait until the end of the year and just look to see how much you made, instead of estimating it in the first quarter and setting up an equal tax payment, you will owe penalties. Alternatively, you will overestimate how much you are going to make, and tie up your own cash by overpaying income tax. This is a big argument for using a corporate structure instead of a sole proprietorship or partnership. Even if you are the only owner, you can structure your company as a corporation.

Applying for credit

Another big argument for using a corporate structure, paying yourself as an employee, is that you will then have a W-2 form. It is much easier to apply for credit, get a telephone installed, buy insurance, and rent an apartment, if you have a W-2 form. You are then an employee of a corporation, with a regular salary, distributed on specific dates. If you don't have a W-2, the fine, well-intentioned employees of big corporations who process those loan applications get confused. When they get confused, they can't check the right boxes on their forms, and you risk being turned down for failure to fit your square peg into their round hole. You will set the salary as low as possible, so that you don't take more money out than the business can afford. If there is more money made, you can pay yourself a bonus at the end of the year. The bonus would then be taxable when it is paid. If you are a corporation of one person, you would most likely pay yourself all the potential profits as a bonus. This prevents them from being double-taxed as both corporate profits and as dividends.

Making Social Security Payments

Both you and your employees need to have social security and medicare payments deducted from your paychecks. You also need to have state and federal income tax deducted, based on your dependents declared on your W-4. Additionally, the corporation or business must submit its own matching contribution for social security and medicare. All of this is a tedious calculation, which you, as the business owner could do yourself, but should not waste your time doing. There is a finite set of forms which must be filled out to satisfy these requirements. You can learn what all of them are at the IRS website.

http://www.irs.gov/businesses/small/article/0,,id=172179,00.html

The best use of your time is to review and moderately understand them. Then either use a simple payroll software package or pay a payroll service to handle it. If you and your spouse will be the only employees, you might want to spend an afternoon learning the forms. Everything you need to know is explained on the IRS website. It is no harder than filling out the forms for the Publisher's Clearinghouse you-may-already-have-won lottery forms, but it is time-consuming and potentially confusing.

Paying consultants

In the past ten years, companies have increasingly moved to paying employees as if they were consultants, in order to avoid paying the company portion of the social security tax. This, of course, means the employee must declare themselves to be operating a sole proprietorship, and pay the company portion themselves at the end of the year. It's like giving them a 7.5% pay cut. IRS rules identify when it is valid to call someone a consultant. They must work for other people, not just for you. They must set their own hours and identify their own tasks within the goal. Many businesses, however, in recent years, have considered it attractive to have employees who get no benefits, no holidays, no vacations, no health insurance, and no pension plan. They are not counted in the unemployment figures. Consultants don't even have to be fired. You can just stop calling them in to work. No matter how attractive that may sound to a penny-pinching entrepreneur, if the person is actually an employee, it is a bad long-term strategy to game the system by calling them a consultant. If you pay someone as a consultant, you must file Form 1099 at the end of the year.

Key points:

1) *You need to get all your employees to submit a W-4 declaring their dependents.*

2) *You need to contact the IRS office and get an Employer Identification Number.*

3) *You need to correctly deduct social security, medicare, state and federal income tax from each employee's paycheck. You need to submit that money, plus the corporate portion of social security and medicare, to the IRS on a specific schedule.*

4) *Quarterly, you need to file reports of what you did to the IRS. Each state also requires reports on varying schedules.*

5) *All of this paperwork is tedious, and initially confusing. It requires a mammoth clerical effort, carried out by a person with a talent for that sort of thing. But it will cause you all kinds of trouble if you don't do it correctly, so you must accept it as a part of doing business, and either hire a good payroll tax service or assign someone on your team to really learn what to do.*

Next Lesson: Module 3: Structuring, Lesson 5: Setting Up Your Website

Module 3: Structuring
Lesson 5: Setting Up Your Website

How to get a website, Choose your domain, How to use your website, Your blog, Your Facebook page, Your Tweets, Selling on eBay and Amazon, Collecting money

Every business needs a website. Your website functions as your brochure, your advertising, your customer information service, and your order form. It can educate persuade, inform, and sell for your business. You don't necessarily have to sell directly from your website, but you do need to provide information about your product offering. Customers today like to research before they buy. If your company is not included in the search results, potential customers will not consider your product in their analysis.

There are many design strategies for your website, and they deserve study before you make your choice. Just like advertising and marketing, there are many ways to present your company and your product, and many ways to make the sale. After you consider your marketing strategy, apply that strategy to your website design.

How to get a website
The Internet is not expensive. It won't be a large budget item in your startup capital. You will need two basic things: a domain name and a hosting service. Your hosting service will most likely make the arrangements for your domain name, so you may find it best to select your hosting service first.

The hosting service essentially rents you a space on their server and connects your space to the Internet on a high speed line. To compete for your business, different hosting services have added features to make you want to choose their product. Among the services you will find offered by hosts are:
- A large number of email accounts available

- Acquisition of a domain name
- Templates to build pre-designed websites that you can customize
- Shopping carts
- Counters to measure your traffic

You can generally get all of this with a nearly-unlimited ability to post your own web pages for between $10 and $30 a month. *You should not pay more to get a website. It is a commodity product.* A few of the web hosting services which offer these basic features are Start Logic, Blue Host, and Verio. Search "web hosting services" and you will find many options. You will need to pay someone to build your site and maintain it, but this is something which is easy to do in-house by your employees or yourself. Do be sure your website has a professional look. Don't overpay for it.

Choose your domain name
The domain name is the web address, or URL, of your site. Get a name which is easy to remember, easy to spell, and represents your company or product well. The best case is to use your company name, assuming you have given your company a good name. There are many websites on the Internet, however, and your company name may already be taken.

> *Tip: Don't just type* **www.my-company-name.com** *into Google to see what happens. There are companies who wait for people to type in a name that is not currently in use. Then, they scoop up the data, and quickly go buy that name. Later, when you try to buy that name for your company, they offer to sell it to you at an inflated price.*

When you are ready, select your web hosting service, and use their online tools to search for a suitable domain name. If their tools tell you that your selection is not available in a 'dot com' version, pass on that name and select another. People will automatically assume that your name ends with 'dot com.' If someone else owns the 'dot com' version, then all of your advertising will point customers to that other website. People will not remember that your website ends with a different suffix, such as dot net or dot biz.

How to use your new website
The website will have explanations and instructions to set up your pages. You will have two basic choices: use a template website builder provided by the hosting service, or write your own web pages and upload them. The free template will give you a limited number of pages. As a start, you might want to put the template up as a placeholder while you are figuring out your web design strategy. It is self-explanatory. You follow the directions and you have a website.

For a longer term strategy, you probably want to build your own site. There are software programs you can buy to help you do that, and there are companies who will offer to design the pages for you. You can also pay a small monthly fee to use your web hosting service's template builder for unlimited pages. If you choose to have someone build the site for you, you will need to spend between $500 and $3,000 to get a decent website. However, if you have any patience or familiarity with computers, it is easy enough to learn HTML code and write your own web pages. Then you can change them whenever you want, and have complete control over the design. There are free lessons on how to write HTML code at http://www.w3schools.com

These lessons are simple enough. If you are planning out your business, time may be abundant but money is tight. Add four weeks to your project plan for learning to use HTML, and write your own website. It is a long term time investment in avoiding thousands of dollars paid to others who will not do exactly what you want done. Alternatively, pick someone on your management team to be the web designer, and assign that as a management responsibility. You don't need to do anything fancy, just basic HTML and CSS (Cascading Style Sheets). Adobe Flash, animation, sound, and movies may be something you want to add later, but they are not necessary in the beginning. In many cases, they detract from the purpose of a business website. The basic shopping cart provided as an add-on to your web hosting service will get you started.

Your Blog

Your website also needs a Blog. A Blog is a special website, different from yours, where you can post thoughts and themes, and readers can comment. The web hosting service will probably include a Blog page, but don't use theirs. Get a different Blog, for free, from one of the free Blog sites. Some possibilities are blogspot.com, wordpress.com, and typepad.com

Set up your free Blog, which is very easy to do, and start posting things to it a few times a week. Be sure to link your Blog to your website. Why? Because search engines give your website more credence if some other website links to you. Also, because search engines give more weighting to pages that change frequently. If your Blog pages change, and if they are related to the important concepts that cause people to buy your product, your Blog might be found by people who are looking for your product. Then they will come to your Blog and find the link to your site. Be certain your Blog topics attract your target customers. Otherwise, you will increase traffic but not convert your traffic into sales.

Your Facebook Page

Your company also needs a Facebook page. You will use this to post announcements about your product and send messages to your existing customers and people who are thinking about being customers. In a sense, it's like a customer service area. Because you want your existing customers to buy more, you can use your Facebook page to offer advanced information and special features, coupons, and discounts for good customers. If you are lucky, the friends of your Facebook friends will notice your postings and sign up to be customers, too. Most business comes from repeat customers and from recommendations from repeat customers. Facebook and other social networking sites behave as a personal service area, where you can interact with your customers and be part of their social circle.

Your Tweets

If and only if your product concept includes a lot of information content, you may want to set up a Twitter account. Tweets are very short messages that can appear on your Facebook pages or in the email accounts and mobile phones of those who choose to follow you. Their purpose is to fit in with the sound-byte society we have created, interrupting the life of people seeking distraction from their jobs. Whether or not you Tweet depends on your personal reaction to the concept of Tweeting. Some people find it distasteful. Others think it's just great to be interrupted. Some look forward to it, so they can stop working. In fact, so much Internet action takes place during work-hours that Hugh Heffner recently introduced a special "workplace safe" site so people didn't have to miss Playboy while they were at the office. How much you choose to take advantage of this phenomenon will be your judgment call as CEO.

Selling on e-Bay and Amazon.com

Your product may be appropriate for sales on other company's websites. Two of the most used sites which sell other people's products are e-Bay and Amazon. Each of these sites has their own rules. These rules are found at the e-Bay and Amazon sites themselves. Look for them and consider whether these sites might be an additional distribution outlet for you.

Collecting money

It's an opportunity lost if you don't sell directly from the website. For this, you will need to set up a means to take credit cards. There are complex options for this. You must be careful about how you do it. Plan time in your business preparations to find and learn your options and set up a merchant account at your bank. There are potential fees and scams that could trick you while you are in the process of choosing vendors for this. Worst case, if you can't get a solid, reputable merchant account at a bank you trust, use PayPal or Google Checkout.

Key points:

1) *You must be included in the conversation online. This is where consideration and analysis of purchasing is being made.*
2) *Websites are cheap and easy to get. Do not overpay for them.*
3) *Your domain name, or URL, should be easy to remember and end in "dot com."*
4) *Website design and maintenance can be done in-house. Your website strategy is too integral to your marketing strategy to farm it out.*
5) *Your Blog, Facebook page, and Tweets are part of your marketing strategy.*
6) *eBay and Amazon.com may be sales outlets for your product. You must research their sites to find out.*
7) *Watch out for scams and fees when you set up your online merchant account. Be careful.*

Next lesson: Module 3: Structuring, Lesson 6: Establishing your accounting system

Module 3: Structuring
Lesson 6: Establishing your accounting system

Getting money out of your business, Recognizing valid business expenses, Overhead, Cost of goods sold, Capital equipment, Earnings before interest and taxes, Rules of thumb

As soon as you establish your business, and file the paperwork with your local, state, and federal government, you need a bank account. The Employer Identification Number, which you got from the IRS, serves as the identifying number on your bank account. Once you set up your business bank account, you must pay your business bills through this account. Don't write some bills from your personal account and some from your business account. If there is not enough money in your business account, and you have to transfer money from your personal account to your business account, you have just invested money in your business. You need your accountant to clearly be able to identify this transaction. You need to get credit for being the investor.

Getting money out of the business

By the same token, don't just write yourself checks from the business account to cover your personal expenses. Money that comes from the business to you is either profit paid from a sole proprietorship to its owner, distributions paid from a partnership to all its owners as defined in the partnership agreement, salary paid from a corporation to its employee, or dividends paid from a corporation to its stockholders. All of these distributions have tax implications. Be very sure you know what those tax implications are before you take the money and spend it. Of course, if you put money into the business and you don't want that money to be an investment, you can take it back out as if you had just made a short term loan. Documents are required to back this up. Cash can't just go from the business to your personal account and back. Money that goes from the business to you has to be identified and categorized appropriately.

Recognizing valid business expenses

You will most likely hire an accounting service for a few hours a month, or purchase an accounting software package for small business use. If you are in the very small planning stages, you might start out with just a spreadsheet until you start bringing in money to pay the accountant. In any case, the first thing you are going to do is define your "chart of accounts."   The Chart of Accounts is your list of how you are categorizing all the items of your revenues and expenses. It is entirely at your discretion to choose these categories. The categories identify bills in a meaningful manner.

> *For example, you might identify your Revenue items first. Maybe you will call Revenue items the "100 series." Arbitrarily, depending on how you believe the numbers will be meaningful to you, you could assign your Chart of Accounts for Revenue like this:*
> *101 – Product A*
> *102 – Product B*
> *103 – Maintenance contracts*
> *104 – Consulting fees*

Whatever you expect to receive in revenue, you assign it a number. Then when the checks come in, your bookkeeper will write that number in your accounting system, along with the date and the amount. This will allow the accounting software to give you reports that summarize "all revenue related to Product A by date."

Then you will move on to your expenses. You will list all the types of expenses you might have. A good way to do that is to separate your fixed overhead expenses from your variable expenses which are associated with each product. You will call the variable expenses associated with each product, your 'Cost of Goods Sold.'

Overhead expenses

Examples of common overhead expenses might be:

201 – Telephone
202 – Internet
203 – Office supplies
204 – Cleaning service
205 – Accounting service
206 – Legal service
207 – Business insurance
208 – Office rent
209 – Utilities
210 – Taxes and license fees
211 – Employee health insurance
212 – Bank fees
213 – Salaries (for overhead employees only)
214 – Social security payments (FICA tax)
215 – Medicare payments
216 – Print Advertising
217 – Printed marketing materials
218 – Internet Advertising
219 – Internet website design consultant

As you pay each bill, you identify the invoice with this Chart of Accounts number. This allows you to query your accounting software to find out how much you paid for each category. In your management decision-making, you must know how much each marketing effort costs to implement. You can define your Chart of Accounts in as much detail as it takes for you, the CEO, to know how you are spending your money. Every marketing activity you do, you must fully understand whether it was worth the effort and cost. You can only do that if you defined your chart of accounts in enough detail to measure it.

Cost of Goods Sold

Some of your costs depend on how many products you are making. You will buy supplies for your inventory, and as you draw them out of inventory, you will apply just the portion of each supply that is used in making that product to your Income

Statement. This is called Cost of Goods Sold. It is important to calculate your cost of goods sold. This is how you know you aren't losing money on each product.

> *For example, if you run a bakery and you use 2 c flour to make each batch of 12 muffins, then every time your "revenue" line indicates that you have sold 12 muffins, your cost of goods sold line will reflect 2 cups of flour, plus the portion of all other supplies and labor which were used to make 12 muffins. However, you probably purchased a 25-lb bag of flour, and the rest of that bag is still in inventory. This is one of the reasons that cash and profit are not the same thing. You paid for 25 pounds of flour, but only 2 cups of flour show on your income statement. The rest of the flour is an asset, held by the business in its inventory. In this case, you may show a profit from selling 12 muffins, but you would not have positive cash, because you spent the cash buying more flour than you needed.*

Capital Equipment

You might also have spent cash buying an oven, baking mitts, pans, and other equipment which you needed for the kitchen to bake the muffins. The capital equipment which you buy is depreciated on your financial records. It doesn't show up all in one year because you can allocate just a portion of the cost to each year. This more accurately reflects your use of the equipment over time. However, the IRS allows businesses to deduct all of the capital equipment bought in one year, up to a dollar limit. This is your option, when you prepare your taxes. It is called a Section 179 deduction. A business owner might choose to take the Section 179 deduction on tax filings, but continue to show an extensive and lengthy depreciation on in-house records. In this case, the in-house books would show a different number for profit than the filings with the IRS. This is completely legal. Business owners may want to take advantage of the lower taxes in one year offered by the Section 179 deduction. However, they may want to show their investors that the business was actually profitable, removing the distortion of the Section 179 from their profits.

Earnings Before Interest and Taxes (EBIT)

Of course, the real earnings from a business are calculated after paying interest and taxes. However, you will often see businesses displaying this EBIT number. This makes it possible to compare companies across an industry. It may distort the performance of the business if you didn't compare it to others in its industry without considering the impact of interest and taxes. Interest and taxes can have widely varying reasons to be highly surprising numbers.

Rules of Thumb

You may not have time, as the CEO of your business, to learn all the accounting and taxation rules. However, it is important for you to be responsibly familiar with the concepts. You will want to set up some "rules of thumb" for your operations, based on your personal understanding of what is important to make your specific business operate efficiently. You will want to know the contribution which each sale makes to your bottom line. This is calculated by subtracting the price of the product from the "cost of goods sold" of each product. This includes the variable labor and supplies which go into each product. You will also want to know the "breakeven" point for each product. That is, how many do you have to sell in order to cover all your fixed costs. (This is the number of products you have to sell before the "contribution" or "margin" covers your overhead expenses.) As the decision-maker, numbers like these should be on the top of your head at all times. If the numbers change, it should be a warning signal that you have to look more closely at operations.

Key points:
1) *Carefully separate your personal accounts from the business accounts.*
2) *You can only get money from the business as a distribution of profit or as a paycheck.*
3) *Good accountants are worth the money.*
4) *Your Chart of Accounts allows you to make sense of your expenditure reporting. It can clarify and improve your management decisions.*
5) *You need to set up some accounting rules of thumb to guide your operational decisions.*

Next Lesson: Module 3: Structuring EXERCISES
Or **Module 4: Marketing, Lesson 1: Reaching Your Target Customer**

Module 3: Structuring EXERCISES

1. Select the type of company you would like to start. Pick a name, a logo, a slogan, and a website address for your company. Does your complete package send a consistent message about your company?

2. Look up the website of your state. Find the rules for starting a company. How hard is it to incorporate?

3. Research web hosting services on the Internet. Which one would you choose for your website? Why?

Join others on the AliceElliottBrown.com Business Blog to discuss your answers.

Module 3: Structuring QUIZ

1. The number which the IRS assigns to a business for the purpose of opening a bank account and paying employees is called the:
   a. Social Security number
   b. Account number
   c. Employer Identification Number
   d. Tax ID

2. In preparing marketing material for your product, your best approach is to emphasize:
   a. The features of the product
   b. What the product does for the customer
   c. The inferiority of competitors
   d. The low price

3. Employers are required to withhold _____ from employee's paychecks.
   a. Social security, medicare, state, and federal income tax
   b. Social security and medicare only. State and federal income tax are optional.
   c. Nothing, withholding is optional.
   d. Social security, medicare, state and federal income tax, retirement benefits, and health insurance.

4. To set up a website, you should first
   a. Write an RFP to select a vendor
   b. Select a domain name
   c. Join a website shopping mall
   d. Select a web hosting service

5. The list of fixed expenses for your business is called your business
   a. COGS
   b. Overhead
   c. Asset
   d. Chart of Accounts

6. The expenses of your business which are dependent on the number of products sold are your:
   a. Cost of Goods

        b. Overhead
        c. Assets
        d. Chart of Accounts

Check your answers on the AliceElliottBrown.com site.

Module 4: Marketing

4-1: Reaching your target customer
4-2: Launching your product
4-3: Differentiating your offering
4-4: Erecting competitive barriers
4-5: Nurturing your competence
4-6: Milking social media

Module 4: Marketing
Lesson 1: Reaching your target customer

Finding your market, Profiling, Meeting customers where they shop, Intercepting at the point of sale

Why would somebody want your product? If you sell a service, the service is your product. All the same questions still apply. The person who chooses to be your customer has a set of specific reasons which motivate them to purchase from you. Before you can plan your marketing campaign, you have to know those reasons. You have to know the motives, the desires, and the triggers of your target customer. What type of person will choose your product? What makes that person open their wallet or pull out their credit card? You have to know where those *types* of people look for products, what phrases and buzzwords appeal to them, what features excite them, and what motivates them to take the action to click the button that says, *"Buy."*

Finding your market
After you know *who* they are, you have to know *where* they are looking for your product. Are they looking in the supermarket? In the shopping mall? In a professional magazine? In a specialty shop? What key words will they use to search the Internet?

After you know *who* they are and *where* they are looking, you have to know *when* they are looking for your product. Are they looking for it every day, week, or month? Are they looking in preparation for a special event, like a wedding or a party? Are they looking when they reach a certain age, when they have a child, or when they get a new job? What do you know about the behavior of your customers? Are they looking at the office or at home?

Finally, you have to know *what* they are looking for and *why* they want it. You've heard the old adage, "sell the sizzle, not the steak." People are not looking for a package of features. They are looking for a solution to some perceived problem which they believe they have. *They want to know what the product will do for them,* not how superior the product is compared to its alternatives. You have to know what problem your customers expect this product to solve.

After you know who, what, when, where, and why, then you are ready to plan your marketing campaign. Your campaign is very simple. You want to find the customers who are looking for the solution to the problem which your product solves. You want to tell them in clear, plain English how this product solves their problem. You want to present the product with a price that is perceived to be a worthy value. You want to make it easy to buy. *There really is nothing more to a marketing campaign than that.*

Profiling
As much as people would like to believe we are each unique and special, the truth is, people can be "profiled" into categories. Groups of people like certain things and have special interests. You need to develop profiles of the categories and groups which want your offering. It works well to give these profiles each a name. They can be names of people you know, or just fake names to help you build a good concept of your types of customers. For example, if you have a business that sells organic food, you might profile your customers like this:

1. *Sharon. Sharon is a Baby Boomer, who is semi-retired. She plants her own garden and researches organic growing practices. She would like to buy all her food from organic sources, but it is very difficult to find organic stores in her rural area. She is likely to use the Internet to make bulk purchases to store in her pantry.*

2. *Ron. Ron is in his late twenties, and single. Mostly, he eats in restaurants and doesn't cook. He is aware of the importance of healthy eating, though, and works out regularly. He would be inclined to buy pre-packaged organic foods on the Internet, if they seemed like they wouldn't be too much trouble.*

3. *Diana. Diana is a young mother with four children. She home-schools the kids, buys at the farmer's market, and cooks from scratch. She constantly searches for fresh ideas and new information about healthy living and family values. She would be inclined to buy both pre-packaged and organic foods in bulk, if they were priced right.*

From these three customer profiles, we see that organic foods can be sold over the Internet in two forms: bulk or pre-packaged. We see that price is important, but only in the sense that the price must reflect the value which the customers attach to organic foods. They do not have to be cheaper than non-organic foods, but they can't be so much more expensive that they do not fit into a family budget. Having identified our customers by profiling, the next question is: where are they looking for products?

With your profiles, you can examine the lives of your various segmented customers, and discover where they shop, or where they look for information about what to buy. Picture Sharon in your head. Do you know a person like Sharon? Can you call her and talk to her about where she looks for organic food? Does she go to Mom's Organic Market? Of course! Does she go to Whole Foods? Yes! Does she read Mother Earth News? Naturally! Can you put ads or brochures or products in any of those places? Maybe. If not, you can definitely make sure that your website mimics some of the message content from those places, so "Sharon" will recognize your message as one she appreciates. You can also make sure the key words that retrieve your website are the same as those that retrieve places Sharon shops.

When you go on to your second targeted customer, Ron, you see that he does not shop at the same places as Sharon. Nor does he read the same magazines. What does he read? He reads online information related to high-performance sports. Ron's goal is different from Sharon's. Sharon is looking to prolong her quality of life and improve her health. Ron is also looking to improve his health, but he wants to excel in athletic performance. He stops in at General Nutrition Center now and then, and he reads Ski magazines online. Ron is a different customer segment, and he will use different search terms when he looks on the Internet for your product.

Diana is way too busy with her young family to drive the extra miles looking for a Whole Foods, so she shops at the local Giant food store. She supplements with the farmer's market in the summertime. You can be at the farmer's market in her town, but you can't be at every farmer's market in every town. Instead, you know you should list yourself with websites like "Local Harvest," which identify organic sources of food.

Each of your customer profiles has different shopping habits and slightly different motives. Their common thread is their concern about health. You know you have to load your website pages with the key words they will be searching.

Intercepting at the point of sale

Customers today use the Internet to compare products, pricing, and features. If they are searching on the Internet, they are close to a purchase decision.

Tip: No matter what else you do for your marketing campaign, you must be included in the Internet search results. You must give your message at the time the customer is looking. Your message has to be simple: "I feel your pain. Here is what solves your problem. Look at what a good value this is. Click here."

After potential customers have received your message, they will be ready to move on to the "validation stage" of their purchase decision. They will search for comparable value, check competitive pricing, and look for customer testimonials and experiences. If you are conducting a robust Internet marketing campaign, your customers will find you everywhere they look. They will consider what others say about your product. They will want to know if it delivers what you promised in your marketing message. If you can get the consensus of customers to agree that it does, they will buy.

That's all there is to it.

Key points:
1) *Sell the sizzle, not the steak. Customers want to know what your product does for them.*
2) *Profiling your customers helps you to guess where they are looking for you.*
3) *Your customers will search for validation through testimonials of others, comparison of pricing and features, and product reviews.*
4) *You have to deliver what your marketing message promises.*

Next lesson: Module 4: Marketing, Lesson 2: Launching your product

Module 4: Marketing
Lesson 2: Launching your product

Shopping as entertainment, Create some urgency, If the ship doesn't sail, Try and try again, When is all lost?

You've identified customer segments.   You know where the customers buy, what they are looking for, and what triggers their decision.   Now the question is: how do you introduce your product to the marketplace and get some "buzz" for it?   You could make it available as soon as it's ready to be shipped, and start distributing your marketing materials. That's a possibility. But, what if nobody notices it for six months? Are you prepared to just sit in the office waiting for somebody to realize it exists and start buying?

Shopping as entertainment
Wouldn't it be better to build up some demand, waiting for the product to be available? How great would it be if the customers lined up at the store, waiting to buy your product the day it hit the shelves?

> *Remember the iPhone4?   Customers stood in lines that curled three times around the block, hoping to be the lucky ones who were honored with the opportunity to buy an iPhone4.*

> *Remember the Harry Potter books?   Bookstores opened at midnight so they could sell the books the day they were available. Customers showed up in the stores to get them at midnight!   The customers dressed up in costumes portraying characters from the books! Buying things is fun! It's entertainment.*

People do shop for entertainment.   Buying something should be an experience in itself.   Many times, people are shopping as therapy, as distraction, or as self-medication from their desperate lives.   People like to have something to look forward to, a "coming attraction." People like anticipation. The anticipation is often sweeter than the event. People also need to talk about your product. The talking is your best advertising method. When your product is new, you have the opportunity to create an event, which could create a 'buzz,' which could get people talking. Don't waste the opportunity to create a 'word of mouth' campaign. Don't seep out into the marketplace. Erupt into it, after a suitable, awaited-for, strawberry-and-whipped-cream-covered, delicious anticipation period.

Create some urgency

To launch your product, get everything ready ahead of time. Have your marketing materials, your final product offering, your packaging, your shipping, your website, and your marketing plan. Collect an email list of potential customers. Write your message out clearly. Pick a date for your 'launch.' Announce the date. Tell retailers your product cannot be sold before that date, but make sure they have product in-house ready to be sold on that date. Throw a party. Send out press releases. Do whatever you can do to create a media event which can cause people to want to be the first on their block to own your product. Think of it like planning any party. You need to send out the invitations early enough for people to schedule it, but not so early they will forget about it. Post the event on your Facebook pages, Twitter about it, and do whatever you think you can do to get people talking. People talk for a while before they buy, so get the talking going. People love to be part of something. They like inclusion. Create a sense of membership.

If the ship doesn't sail

If you worked hard on your product launch, but your ship didn't sail, you must analyze why not. Did the launch preparation fail? Or did the product fizzle? Products that do not "launch" may never "catch the wind." You are not in control of the market. In choosing your product, you looked for a product which solved a perceived need, responded to a specific customer base, appealed to a certain target profile, and offered a proposed value. If you carefully introduced this message with a sense of urgency to the right customer segment, but they stayed home on the day of your party, you have a serious problem. Don't spend any more money until you have figured it out.

Try and try again
Find out what went wrong. Fix it. Launch again. Call it the new product, version 2, an advanced, enhanced, super-duper whizz bang. Talk to customers. Offer specials, discounts, coupons, and deals. The key is: you must know what your customers want and what drives them to buy. It is hard, sometimes, for an entrepreneur to understand that the market is a wild, untamed, uncontrolled animal. You do not control it. *You only offer it food and see if it eats.* Trend-setters are merely those who notice where the crowd is heading, and run out in front of it. You succeed as an entrepreneur when you see a market need and fill it. You cannot fill a need if it does not exist.

When is all lost?
If your product was carefully researched and you understood your target market, all is not lost. You can tweak and adjust your product until it catches on with the market base. Persistence will allow you to find the right combination that starts the sales growth. This is just part of the iterative nature of marketing. Feedback, feedback, feedback. Change until the market responds. Be all your customers want you to be.

There are times when an entrepreneur becomes so invested in an idea that he or she feels driven to implement it in the face of all adversity. Despite market feedback which rejects it, the entrepreneur sometimes carries stalwartly on, continuing to push a wet noodle uphill with her nose.

Recognize defeat. If the market does not support an idea, close the project down. Cut your losses. Move on to the next idea. Salvage what you can, and learn from your mistakes. Most importantly, do not invest your personal identity into any product concept. If an idea does not catch on in the market, have the courage to scrap it and try another path. Successful managers run businesses; they don't proselytize ideals. Pay attention to market feedback and do whatever works.

Key points:
1) *Customers respond to anticipation, urgency, and entertainment.*
2) *People like to feel membership and inclusion. You can create that in your product launch.*
3) *If your product fails to launch, you must find out what is wrong and correct it.*
4) *Businesses are built on filling a market need. The market is the final decision-maker on what it needs.*
5) *Try and try again, but don't try the same way twice.*
6) *Do what works. Stop doing what isn't working.*

Next lesson: Module 4: Marketing, Lesson 3: Differentiating your offering

Module 4: Marketing
Lesson 3: Differentiating your offering

What is different about your product, Making your name special, Using social media, Adding your two cents, The many ways to be special

You've identified your target market segments and profiled your customers. You know them. You know why and how they buy. You've invited them to your product launch party. They are talking about you. You have to know what they are saying. If they say bad things, your business is in trouble. The bad things they say don't have to be true. If they say them, true or not, you are knocked for a loop. People who like your product are less likely to talk about it than people who are angry or people who feel cheated. You need to be sure you have your customer service, your product support, and your product features in good shape before you launch. Dissatisfied customers can damage your business fatally. You, as the CEO, need to keep an "ear to the ground" with your customers, to make sure they are happy with your product and your product support.

What is different about your product?
In the messages people spread about your product, you hope they will tell others why your product is different from its competitors. Of course, before that happens, you have to make sure your product really is different from its competitors. It has to be different in a meaningful way, a way that is perceived to be valuable by your target market segments. If Bob's walking sticks were just run-of-the-mill varnished wood, why would anybody pay twice the price for them? Whatever your distinctive competence is, it needs to be both reflected in your product line and communicated to your target market. It has to be part of your marketing message.

> *Remember the television commercial where the little kid puts on a pair of sneakers, runs around the room, and declares those sneakers to be "faster?" It's funny. It grabs*

our attention. We know those sneakers are not faster. Yet, the message we receive is that the shoes fit better. If the shoes fit better, they will make the little kid run faster. It's a great message.

In just a few words and a quick visual, we have received a message that is believable. Now comes the hard part. We can remember that message, but forget the name of the sneakers in question. When you put together your marketing message, don't let that happen. The name of your product has to be indelibly imprinted into the message.

Making your name special

Your product has to be "branded," or differentiated in the mindshare of your customers. It has to be imprinted in their minds, so that they associate the special and unique qualities of your product with your name. Think about the commercial that shows a group of people, and the leader says, "When I say Hilshire, you say Farm." If you hear that enough times, you will not be able to think the word "farm" without thinking "Hilshire." Make the customers unable to think of the type of your product without thinking of the product name. Our minds work that way. We associate. If you could get your target customers to think of your product name every time they turned on the water to take a shower, wouldn't that be great? Associating your product name with some daily, routine activity, can make them search you out and choose to buy.

How do you do that? Television commercials are the most effective way to create that association. If you are a small business without the budget for television, you are going to have to do it using the tools of the Internet. Fortunately, we have YouTube.

Using Social Media

You need your customers to be your advertising medium. You need them to tell their friends about your product. Using a Blog, Facebook, Twitter, YouTube, and other social networking sites, you can achieve the mindshare that can compete with television advertising.   You figure out what makes your product special, why it is superior to its competition, and what value it has to solve a problem for your target market segments. You put that message out there in a catchy, sing-song video, and let your customers spread it.   Videos can also serve to educate your customers about your product and offer them support.

Whether you participate in social media or not, your customers are doing it. Millions of people are posting short messages every few minutes, literally about nothing, and often referring to commercial products.

> *They are posting: "Went to the pool and tried out my new Kleenex bathing suit." They are posting: "Can't wait to get a margarita at Casa Honcho tonight."   They are posting: "Stood in line all night to buy an iPhone4." They are posting: "Got ripped off at Billy Bob's. Lousy service."*

Like it or not, they are telling their friends about products and companies.   They are making recommendations and giving testimonials. They are *reviewing* your company! Worse, they are reviewing it to people who are validated as their "friends." These reviews are posting on their friends' pages, where friends of their friends can see them.   You may not like it, but you can't do anything about it. Don't stick your head in the sand. This is where products are being reviewed and recommended.   No matter how distasteful you may find it, no matter how foolish you may consider it, no matter how disturbing it is to you personally, too many people are doing it for you to ignore.

Adding your Two Cents

When you can't beat 'em, your only choice is to join 'em. If your customers are out there on social networking sites talking about your company, you need to be there to defend yourself. You need a Twitter account and a Facebook fan page, so your supporters can speak up.   It can be a customer service area, where you address complaints and set them right. This is your reputation, your differentiation, and your opportunity to present your company as a participator, a responder, and a collaborator in filling the market need.

The many ways to be special
Your product could be special because it has a unique feature, unique design, or unique application. It could be special because it has better service, better support, or better delivery terms. It could be special because it includes information, exclusivity, or membership in a club. There are many alternative ways to be better than the competition. It only matters that the people who are in your target market consider it to be better based on their value system. People will be loyal to a brand they trust. If you establish your product as superior in their minds, it will take an extraordinary event to cause them to switch brands. People don't usually care enough to take the risk of brand-switching, once they have been convinced that they have found a good product. Your job, as CEO, is to convince your target market that they have made the right choice in choosing to solve their problem by using your product. You have to point out to them why they are special for having chosen *you*. If you are out there with them, marketing on the Internet, they will meet you when they research and consider their purchase.

Key points:
1. *You need to tell people what makes them so special to have chosen you.*
2. *Social media on the Internet impacts people during their consideration of the purchase. It is part of their investigation and research. You need to be there for them.*
3. *Your fan pages in social media act as customer service reps.*
4. *Your company needs to be perceived as a responsive collaborator which fills a market need.*

Next lesson: Module 4: Marketing, Lesson 4: Erecting competitive barriers

Module 4: Marketing
Lesson 4: Erecting competitive barriers

Examples of barriers, Protecting your position, Customer retention, New product introduction

Competitive barriers are a wonderful thing. They prevent new entries into an industry. They place obstacles around customers, so that new competitors are unable to get them to switch. People are not inclined to change brands without a strong motive, so barriers can be as simple as a strong branding message.

Examples of competitive barriers

- **Heavy costs for equipment purchases.** If a lot of equipment is needed to enter an industry (for example, an oil drilling rig), it is very hard to justify starting up a new business in that industry.

- **Difficult regulatory processes.** If you need to jump through a lot of legal and regulatory hoops, it is unlikely that a new business will enter an industry. (For example, new television channels or new telephone companies.)

- **Major, large competitors already entrenched.** If there are very big companies already dominating consumer marketshare, it will be difficult to carve out a niche. (For example, the Big Box retailers such as Big Lots, Target, K-Mart/Sears, Wal-Mart.)

- **Domination of the distribution channels.** Who is going to enter a market to compete with Federal Express, UPS, and the US Post Office? The amount of capital and advertising required would prohibit new entries. By the same token, if a company controls or owns the only method available to deliver a product, others cannot compete. An example would be vending machines for soft drinks. If the vending machines are owned by Coca Cola, Pepsi Cola cannot sell their product line in those machines.

- **Strong branding**. Customers are generally loyal to a brand they like. If a strong competitor has achieved a dominant market share, new entrants will have to make their product significantly different in order to carve out a niche market.

Of these, strong branding is the only one readily available for a small business to use. Thanks to the Internet and social media, it is possible for a small company to enter a market, capture a dominant position in a narrowly defined niche segment, establish mindshare of its target customers, and create the monopoly position for that narrowly defined segment. This is the best way to protect your pricing position and prevent your product price from eroding to a commodity.

Protecting your position

How does a company go about protecting its brand? The steps are:

1. *Define your target segment as narrowly as possible.* Identify the customers who are in your segment. For example, "sports equipment" is a large category, best served by large retailers like The Sports Authority. But "high-end fishing equipment for enthusiasts" is a narrowly defined niche market which can be fully dominated by a small business.

2. *Make a name for yourself in that narrowly defined category.* Consistently present high quality products and services which satisfy customers fully. Brand, brand, brand. Use your name, associate it with high quality, and toot your own horn at every opportunity.

3. *Hold your prices high.* Do not succumb to the myth that price is the issue. Value is the issue. Value is the perception of worth. Be very sure you are creating the perception that your product is worth its price.

4. *Beat off the competition with a stick.* Make your product significantly better in some manner. Point out your customer's superior judgment for choosing your brand. If necessary, drop prices just long enough to drive a new competitor who tries to enter the market out of business. If you have to engage in a price war, dip your prices so low that it puts your competitor in a position of needing to drop even lower. Then, change your product line and introduce a better product at a higher price. This makes the lower priced product belonging to your competitor the "old" version. If you do this skillfully, you can drive any competitors out of your market space.

5. *Grab your market share and hold it.* Customer retention is far more important to your business than constantly acquiring new customers. It costs a lot to get a new customer, but most of your business comes from repeat customers. When someone becomes your customer, treat them like royalty. Make them care about your company. Make them feel like geniuses for choosing to buy your product. Reward them for their continuing loyalty. Bring them into your inner circle.

6. *Pay attention to customer feedback.* If you lose a customer, find out why. Change your behavior so it doesn't happen again.

If you build a strong brand, nurture your customer base, and establish a relationship with your target segment, you will protect your revenue stream from erosion by a competitor.

Customer retention

It is far more costly to acquire a new customer than to retain an old one. The barriers you erect keep your customers from switching brands. Once someone has become a customer, your barriers fall into the areas of customer service, product quality, and perceived value. These are generally the purview of the operations department, rather than marketing. Some companies assign a Product Manager, whose responsibility includes tracking customer satisfaction. As the CEO, it is up to you to check customer satisfaction regularly. This is another reason to monitor your online reputation.

New product introductions

You have to stay ahead of your competition in introducing advanced and updated features. Even your most loyal customers will leave you if a competitor brings an advanced product online which has a higher perceived value. Current customers should get a "heads up" about your new product schedule, an advance preview, or a special price to upgrade to the latest versions.

Key points:
1) *Branding is the primary competitive barrier available to small companies.*
2) *You protect your price position by defining your market niche narrowly, and dominating the mindshare of those customers whose problems are solved by your specific product.*
3) *Customer retention is the key business goal. It depends on delivery of a product which meets the expectations set by the marketing message.*
4) *Customer satisfaction is the responsibility of the CEO.*
5) *New product introductions are a requirement for market share retention. Existing customers should be included as valued partners who get a "heads up" when new products are coming.*

Next lesson: Module 4: Marketing, Lesson 5: Nurturing your competence

Module 4: Marketing
Lesson 5: Nurturing your competence

People choose to contribute, Company culture, Hiring good people, Manage customer relationships, Track backroom functions, Mechanize routine processes

You have worked to make your product unique, special, and different.   Your company, too, has many aspects of uniqueness. That unique aspect of you, the CEO, has to transfer to a uniqueness of your whole company.   The question becomes: how do you get the special talents which caused you, the CEO, to form this company, to be the talents of the company itself, instead of just your personal contribution as an individual? The fact is, you can't run this whole company by yourself, with just your brilliant ability.   Somehow, some way, you have to get a group of people to run it using their ability.   The last thing you want, as a CEO, is to do all the work yourself, paying your people to attend. You need to be a leader, so your followers can fulfill their potential.

People choose to contribute
It may seem counter-intuitive, but people are not happy sitting around doing nothing. They actually do want to feel part of a meaningful effort.   The happiest people at work are those who believe they are working hard for a good cause. You motivate them by giving them control over their own small piece of the effort, within established boundaries. You focus the assignment on a tangible result, moreso than on a process. People have differing cognitive styles. If you specifically define how to do something in too much detail, you turn all your jobs into clerical jobs. Studies show that clerical jobs are more stressful than executive jobs, because the lack of control over the work effort raises anxiety.

Company culture
How do you get people to do what you want? Every group develops its own group culture. Members of each human group

sanction each other's behavior to establish and enforce group norms. This begins in the family, when mothers teach their children to chew with their mouth closed. Some cultures teach that it is polite to burp after eating. Others teach that it is impolite to burp in public. Cultures define their own norms, and enforce those norms among their members. This extends to ethnic groups, schools, churches, clubs, and community organizations. The workplace group is no exception. Humans teach their group members the accepted behavior of that group. To a large extent, the group norms of your company will reflect the behavior people observe from *you*, their leader.

The leader's example will permeate the group. If the leader is dishonest, the employees will steal. The values which employees see enacted by their leader are those they will adopt. Your job, as the leader, is to set the values, pursue them passionately, focus efforts on the goal, and provide the employees with the resources they need to succeed at their tasks. In one sense, you work for them. You get them the resources they need to accomplish their mission. To gain their respect, you must communicate the goal, and ask them what barriers you might remove for them, and what resources you need to provide. You must hear their answers.

Hiring good people

Some people don't respond to the group sanctions. It is worth the effort to extensively screen candidates to hire only people who will fit with your company culture. It is also important to act quickly to remove an employee who is disrupting the culture. The culture of your group is its value system. A broken value system is hard to mend.

The people you hire are each going to make a personal decision about whether they choose to follow you as their leader. If they say no, you don't lead. Leaders can't declare themselves the boss. Nobody can be the boss without the employee's permission. Followers are the decision-makers about who will be their leader. It is the person who picks up the hammer to pound the nail who has the power to decide whether or not the house will be built. Respect that power, and realize your dependence on your followers. You cannot be a team by yourself.

Manage your customer relationships

The key to transferring your personal enthusiasm for the business into company-wide vision may be to display your respect for customers. After you have instilled the value of respect for customers, then you can install guiding software for customer relationship management (CRM.) CRM software sets up a database on your company network. The database contains all customer contact information, including order history and contact information. Every time someone from the company speaks to that customer, they write up notes about what was said and add the notes to the database. That way, if the customer calls in, whoever answers the phone can pull up all the historical interactions which anyone in the company had with that customer. It keeps the customer from repeating their problem every time they call in. Of course, the software is only as good as the discipline that requires your employees to keep the database updated. The software works as a tool to implement the management attitude. If your employees believe you have a bad attitude toward customers, software will not fix that problem.

Track your backroom functions

Your customer contact and all your support activities leave an impression on your customers. They know if your service is good, your quality is high, and your employees respond to their concerns. They know if your billing system is out of whack, or your shipping and logistics are in disarray. Fortunately, even small companies can install a low cost Enterprise Software System, which will tie together your CRM, your ordering and shipping, your management of customer returns, your support system, your billing, your accounting, and even your payroll. One of these systems that is affordable for small business is NetSuite. http://www.netsuite.com/portal/home.shtml

Another popular enterprise system includes SalesForce.com from SAAS. Forbes has written about the virtues of SAAS here. http://www.forbes.com/2008/05/21/netsuite-salesforce-software-ent-tech-cx_bm_0520bmightysaas.html

Mechanize routine processes

If you have a good attitude established, and you just need the routine processes to be tracked and standardized, software has merit to help you. Enterprise systems take some work to implement in your company. By automating and mechanizing the routine processes which run your business, however, you leave your employees free to put their innovative effort into their jobs. Let employees be your real support system. Let them want to contribute. Appreciate their efforts. It's the only way you will be able to let go of the reins enough to have a family life.

Key points:
1) *Leaders help others be all they can be. You are not a team alone.*
2) *Your job is to set the goals, remove the barriers, and provide the resources. Your team must build the house.*
3) *The hiring process is a critical component of your success. Hire people who will fit your group culture.*
4) *Your attitude toward customers will be observed and mimicked by your employees.*
5) *Backroom office functions can be mechanized to allow your people to succeed.*

Next lesson: Module 4: Marketing, Lesson 6: Milking social media

Module 4: Marketing
Lesson 6: Milking Social Media

No more pop-ups, People do want ads, First you have to Blog, Join the conversation

Social media has become a phenomenon of the e-commerce world. It has changed marketing in the same way the telephone changed communication. By social media, we mean social networking sites such as Linked-In, Facebook, and MySpace. We also include sites which spread a "buzz," such as Twitter, Plurk, Flickr, and Blogs of every form. Print advertising cannot compete with a viral YouTube which can be spread around the world by people sending an email to their "joke list." The benefits of getting website visitors to recommend you to their friends by "Liking" you on Facebook are too wonderful to describe.

It's like compound interest. One person tries your product and likes it. That person has 324 friends on Facebook. Each of their friends has another 100 unique friends, which do not overlap. In no time at all, your name has been exposed to thousands of people, with a positive recommendation. Make no mistake about it, a negative comment on a social networking site carries much more weight than a positive comment. Be extremely respectful of the power of these Internet networks. There are some who believe the social networking power of the Internet elected the President of the United States. You want to use this social media to your business advantage. How do you do it?

No more pop-ups
In the beginning of the Internet (which was about 1992), companies would paste banner ads on their sites, and buy the right to open up a pop-up ad when you visited a site. When you closed down your browser after surfing, there would be that annoying pop-up, getting right in your face. Consumers didn't like it, and soon browsers came equipped with "pop-up blockers." Pop-up blockers try to prevent ads from appearing.

The lesson learned? People don't want ads to get in their way. Ads can't be "in your face." The question for a marketer is: do people want advertising at all? Or, is it just a fact of life that people detest being bothered by ads, so it doesn't matter if the ads are annoying, just send them out anyway?

People do want ads!
When people have a problem, they are looking for a solution. They want information about how to solve their problem. They will look for that information, and in these days, they will look on the Internet. They will put search words into Google, or Yahoo, or whatever search engine they use. They will describe their problem, and hope to find some way to solve it. This is when you need to be there with your message. You have to be there for them, with the explanation of how your product benefits them, at the time they are looking for it. You can try to get your company's website to come up with the right key words, on the first page, but getting positioned on the first search page may be very hard to do. This is where social media comes in.

"I can check it out online."
In the old days, about five years ago, people may have acted on a television commercial, a radio spot, or a magazine ad.   If they didn't know anyone who used the product, they might have tried a product out, to see for themselves, based on the recommendation of an advertisement. But now? Before anyone buys, they Google. They check the competitor's offerings. They look for testimonials. They search for complaints. They may post a question to their Facebook friends, to see if anyone has anything to say about it. The friends of their friends may answer. They might stumble across a Blog comment or a YouTube demonstration.   Social media makes the whole world a small town. Gossip is everywhere.

First, you have to Blog
Setting up your own Blog, about topics related to things your customers care about, helps to increase your website's position

in search engines. Actually, it's the Blog that has the higher position, and then your blog links to your site, driving traffic to the site after people conclude that your blog is worthwhile.

After you blog, then you Tweet. Tweeting, using Twitter, allows you to build up a following of people who want to hear from you about things that are important to them. Remember, nobody cares about you or your product. They only want you to Tweet about things that interest them. Where your product's benefits interest them, then you have a sale.

After you Tweet, you can collect some Facebook fans, on your Facebook fan page. You can hope your fans will recommend you to their friends and the friends of their friends, so that people can "like" you. Usually, they like things that entertain them, which is why you need to post a few YouTube videos and some catchy tunes.

Join the conversation
Like it or not, your customers are talking about you online. Your choice to ignore their comments will be seen as arrogance. They need you to participate, to be sensitive to their concerns, and to respond. If they complain, they need you to tell them what you are doing to fix the problem. All of this can get complex. You might have to hire someone just to do online marketing. But, done right, it can be vastly more cost-effective than printed media.

Key points:
1) *Social media is a powerful force which impacts sales.*
2) *Online research is the new point of sale.*
3) *Online marketing is complex and requires skill and focus.*
4) *Like it or not, your customers are discussing you online. You don't control what they say, but you can join the conversation.*

Next lesson: Module 4: Marketing EXERCISES
Or **Module 5: Operating, Lesson 1: Offices and Equipment**

Module 4: Marketing
EXERCISES

1. Get free accounts at Facebook, Twitter, Plurk, and YouTube. Examine the sites and learn how they operate. Observe what people do on them. Consider how you could fit them into your marketing mix.

2. Using key word searches, look for Blogs that are about topics which your customer base might read. Read the comments on the Blogs and become familiar with how your target customers feel about those topics. Consider what type of Blog you might operate for your business.

3. Write a profile of each of your target customer segments. Describe how your customers might behave, where they might find your product, and what benefits they would want.

Join others to discuss your answers on the AliceElliottBrown.com Business Blog

Module 4: Marketing QUIZ

1. What is the best reason you should profile your target customer segments?
    a. To help you find them so you can deliver your message.
    b. To divide them into stereotypes
    c. For categorization in your files.
    d. You should not. Profiling is illegal.
2. Why should you announce your product before it is available?
    a. You should not. It annoys people to find out it is not ready.
    b. To build anticipation and get sales in the queue.
    c. The IRS requires it.
    d. To bring in cash before you ship the product.
3. What would cause a customer to switch brands?
    a. Lower prices
    b. New features
    c. A perception that something is extraordinary about the new brand.
    d. Gossip and rumor that denigrates the old brand.
4. What is the best way to protect your product pricing from erosion to competitors?
    a. Dominate a narrowly defined niche market.
    b. Be the lowest priced product.
    c. Be the highest quality product.
    d. Provide good customer service.
5. To free your employees time so they can contribute their best work, the entrepreneur might choose to:
    a. Install software for routine processes
    b. Hire illegal aliens for the grunt work
    c. Do everything himself or herself
    d. Outsource the routine tasks
6. The best use of social media is to:
    a. Deliver your message in more forms
    b. Create a "buzz" about topics that lead traffic to your website

c. Make yourself feel good because you get more email
d. Waste your time so you don't have to get any work done

Check your answers at AliceElliottBrown.com

Module 5: Operating

5-1: Offices and equipment

5-2: Staff

5-3: Inventory

5-4: Customer relationships

5-5: Accounting

5-6: Strategic relevance

Module 5: Operating
Lesson 1: Offices and equipment

Working from your house, Upgrading to an executive suite, Moving into a business incubator, Renting an office, Equipment tax, Lease vs buy

At first, there are so many planning tasks to do. You have market research, business planning, looking for suppliers, raising funds, putting your team together. You can easily spend months doing this work. Until you need to meet with customers, you don't need to spend money on an office.

Working from your house

If this business is a startup, you can work out of your house. If you are building a product, you can set up your basement for initial inventory. You will need prototypes, so you might as well try to build them yourself. To reduce the risk of your business, you will want to test your processes for manufacturing, as well as your market for the finished product. Setting up in your basement or garage can work well until you have the steady income to commit to an office lease. If you are not allowed, by local ordinance or homeowner's association rules, to operate a business from your home address, you can plan to move out as soon as you start making money. Until you get some cash flow going, how is this a business? It's a hobby. What are you doing except wishful thinking and playing around with ideas? Until your business makes money, work from your basement.

The next step up is to get a mailbox account for your business address, and sign up for an answering service or a VoIP service over the Internet for your telephones. The mailbox account can avoid the problem of having the neighbors notice that the UPS truck makes a pickup at your house every day. The telephone service can give your customers the impression that they are dealing with a larger company. When choosing a telephone service, you can get an answering service. This provides a "receptionist" to answer the phone and take a message for you.

If you are actually available at the time, the receptionist will put the call through to your house, or put the person through to a voicemail box set up for this purpose. The customer thinks they are talking to a normal office with a receptionist, rather than an answering service that transfers calls to your house.

The same thing happens when you use a VoIP service, like OneBox.com. Instead of a human receptionist, the caller gets a recorded message asking them to select 1 for Sales, 2 for Service, or 3 for the President (or whatever you decide to record.) You can forward the different numbers to different people on your team. Your employees can all work out of their respective houses. The customer will get the impression they have called the receptionist of a large company. You can set up a virtual operation for your company, with each person working out of their own houses, using Internet and VoIP phone services.

Upgrading to an "Executive Suite"
In cities, you are likely to find companies whose business is to provide you with a small office space. It might be just one office for one person. All the companies in the building get their name on the lobby directory. They all share the same receptionist and lobby for visitors. Then the various businesses can sign up for times to use the joint conference room. This way, your business can meet with potential customers or make business deals, while appearing to actually have a suite with a lobby, a receptionist, and a conference room.

Entering a "Business Incubator"
Some local governments participate in programs which provide business incubators. An incubator helps a startup company by offering discounted office rent, a shared secretary, shared copying machines, shared conference rooms, and access to legal, accounting, and business advisors. Participants in these incubators may also have access to state grants which encourage job creation. Part of your business planning process could include investigation of your local government incentives for new business. You may be able to find this on your state

website for commerce. Contact the Economic Development Authority in your local county.

Renting an office

It might feel good to see your company name on an office door, have your secretary sitting at her desk outside your office, and park your car in a space that says Reserved on it. You might convince yourself that you are working more productively because you have a place to go to work in the morning. Until you have a real need to bring employees into the office, meet with customers in your own space, and store inventory beyond the limits of your garage, it is wise to resist the urge to commit to a long term lease. Most office space requires a 2 – 5 year lease. There may be build-out costs to arrange the space according to your needs. You will also have the costs of installing a telephone system, buying furniture, and turning on the electricity. It might be too much too soon. It might break the bank for your company. You don't need to do it before you have the cash flow. Wait until you are solid enough financially to commit to office space.

Equipment tax

Some local governments tax the equipment you buy for your business. This alone may be reason to lease instead of buying. You might also choose used equipment. While a new business may happily take the Section 179 deduction for furniture and computers and copiers, this can backfire when the local county sends you a tax bill for your "Machine and Tool Tax." It may be better to purchase things in your own name, for your personal use, and then lease them to the business. Each decision will depend on the specifics of the costs and the taxes over time. You will also have to analyze the consequences of "make vs buy" for each product. There is not one answer for all situations.

Lease vs Buy

Cash is king in a new small business. Although you may clearly understand how to calculate the benefits of leases, compared to purchases, small business often needs to watch cash more than it needs to measure profit. Remember, in your cash budgeting, that leased equipment is a possible alternative to spending cash on hand.

Key points:
1) *In your business planning, you can save money by postponing office rental until you really need it.*
2) *Executive suites, telephone answering services, business incubators, and mailing services may be able to fill your needs until you are financially stable.*
3) *Cash budgeting may suggest leasing equipment, even if the profit calculation tells you to purchase.*
4) *Business equipment is sometimes taxed by the local government.*

Next lesson: Module 5: Operating, Lesson 2: Staff

Module 5: Operating
Lesson 2: Staff

Lawyers and accountants, Vice presidents, Selecting team members, Hiring employees, Benefits, Staffing practices over time

You are your first staff member. Your first question for yourself is: what tasks do I do well, and what tasks should I hire someone else to do? You will look at yourself critically, and honestly figure out your weaknesses, so you can assign your weak areas to someone else.

Lawyers and accountants
Your first tasks to farm out are the legal and accounting services. These tasks require dedicated professionals. You will hire someone to do those, and put some amount of money into your business plan to pay a few hours a month for accounting. For legal services, you will need some advice at startup. You will also need some advice to sign contracts or make agreements, as you progress in your plans. Of course, if you take any investment money, you will need legal advice for that process.

Your accountant should have opinions. If accounting were straight-forward, standardized, no-brainer bean-counting, you could use accounting software and be done with it. Accounting is not bean counting. Management decisions have implications for tax treatment and investment options. You want an accountant who understands those implications and will advise you about the consequences of your decisions before you commit to a path.

Your lawyer, however, can safely keep his or her opinions private. Many inexperienced managers make the mistake of asking their lawyers how to manage their businesses. *This results in marketing material that sends chills down the spine of potential customers.* Your lawyer's job is to advise you on the legal means of accomplishing what you want done. *Nothing else.* You tell your lawyer what you want done; your lawyer tells you how to legally do it. Keep the lawyer in the lawyer box. Bring him out when needed. Put him back after use.

Vice Presidents

Somebody has to be in charge of marketing, operations, technology, finance, human resources, facilities, and the janitorial service. Depending on what your business does, some of those are more important than others. First, you decide which of those you are handling all on your own. Your strongest point is likely to be either marketing or operations. Those are the two areas that have to be covered at the highest management levels. If you have a partner, your partner has to be strong in the areas where you are weak. Otherwise, your partnership may be less than useful. Two partners who share the same strengths may introduce more conflict than synergy. If you have a management team, where a group of people are all founders, you can still form either a partnership or a corporation. That decision is based on long-term intention and tax consequences. Founding members are owners in the company but they need not all be part of the management team. When you choose your management team, you must choose based on ability to do the job.

Based on the abilities and inclinations of your management team, you will divide up the responsibilities for all the functions of the company. Then you will start writing job descriptions. Your top Vice Presidents, no matter how many there are, should write their own job descriptions first. They will probably resist this and tell you it is not necessary. It is necessary, however, because until the team clearly defines responsibilities, someone will always misunderstand. By writing out detailed job descriptions, sharing them with the team, and discussing them, you can find out where the overlaps and conflicts lie. Right at the beginning, you can come to an agreement about who has which responsibilities.

Selecting team members

If your founding management team lacks some specific capability, you can consider whether you will bring in another founder, or hire a plain old employee with no stake in the company. If the capability is mission critical, you may want to offer an ownership stake to a person with serious experience and background in that skill. It may take the incentive of ownership to attract someone with the right skills. Your company cannot offer the stability and security of an established firm, so an ownership incentive may be required.

On the other hand, giving away pieces of your company to strangers can be dangerous. You must structure the deal so that the person does not get any piece of the company until they have been with the company for a certain period of time. The name for this is "vesting." Do not give away pieces of your company to strangers without writing a period of "vesting" time into the deal. They might not work out as employees. You don't want them to walk away with ownership if that happens. If possible, avoid offering any employee a contract. Let all employees work "at-will." You don't want to be forced to buy someone out if they are doing a bad job. Your founders will have ownership. This should be the extent of their contracts.

Hiring employees

For non-owner employees, you need a solid hiring process. It is an extraordinary expense to hire someone who doesn't work out. You waste your time training them. You waste your company's time and money while they do a bad job. You risk your company's reputation if they represent your company poorly. You may lose new sales and existing customers. After it's all over, you risk having them sue you for some perceived violation of employment law. It is worth spending considerable effort to hire the right person in the first place.

To select the right employee, you need every member of your management team to agree that this person will fit in with the group. It has to be unanimous. "Fit with the group" is more important than background and skills.   First, from the resumes you receive, bring in the top few candidates to interview with each manager.   Because all the candidates invited are fully qualified, the final decision can be made based on who is best-liked by the team. When the team agrees on one candidate, invite that candidate to have dinner with all of you. If you can't stand spending a few leisure hours over dinner with this person, imagine how horrible it will be to have to work with them day in and day out. Finally, after you have agreed to hire the person, check their references. Few people will be foolish enough to give you a name for a reference who will say negative things.   If that happens, consider carefully whether you should hire that person.   Bring in the next best person from your list and try again.

Benefits

Your small company has to work as a well-functioning team. Be careful not to create an environment with two classes of team members. If the founders and the non-founder employees turn into an "us versus them," you will get passive-aggressive behavior from your staff. Make sure you show appreciation for the work your team produces.

> *Tip: If your company is a corporation, you can set benefit plans in place. You have the option to create different plans for top management than for non-ownership staff.   If you do that, keep it quiet and discrete. Do not rub the noses of your staff in their different treatment. Be sure to provide at least health insurance, holiday pay, vacation pay, and sick pay for everyone.   Team-building activities such as company picnics, birthday cakes in the break room, family day at the amusement park, and holiday brunches are far more important to team spirit than some hard-charging, rational entrepreneurs might think.*

Staffing practices over time

Remember that laying off people and firing people has a deep and lasting impact on the rest of your staff. Do not hire before you must. If you get into the position that you must lay off an employee, those who are not laid off will start looking for a new job. Productivity in the company will drop dramatically. Morale will fail. Plan to hire only as you are sure you can support the team.

Key points:
1) *Accountants and lawyers have their place in your business. Keep them in it. Decision-making and its burdens belong to you.*
2) *Your founding partners will hopefully all have different strengths.*
3) *Job descriptions help to eliminate conflict.*
4) *Let stock ownership for employees vest over time.*
5) *"Fit with the group" is a critical hiring criteria.*
6) *Benefit plans and team-building activities are part of your staffing strategy.*
7) *Laying off people will cripple team morale. Avoid hiring until you are sure there is a sustainable need.*

Next lesson: Module 5: Operating, Lesson 3: Inventory

Module 5: Operating
Lesson 3: Inventory

Overhead, FIFO/LIFO, Cash is not profit, Just-in-time inventory, Requirements planning software

You can think of inventory as your potential for sales. Small business managers generally work on "rules of thumb." Rule of thumb, you should sell things for twice what you paid for them. If you can. If you are the manufacturer, you need to get double your costs when you sell to a retailer. If you are a retailer, you need twice that again when you sell to the customer. In general, the production costs of a manufactured product are usually less than 25% of that product's end price to the consumer. They have to be. The costs of marketing, packaging, shipping, distributing, and delivering are the primary costs of doing business.

> *Tip: Here is everything a small business owner needs to know about inventory.*
> > *1. It needs to be sold, not stored. Your worst nightmare is buying inventory that customers don't want.*
> > *2. Its costs change over time. The inventory you buy in January may have a different cost to you than the same inventory purchased in July.*
> > *3. It exists on your balance sheet, but not on your income statement. It impacts cash but not profit.*

Overhead
If you are a manufacturer, part of your inventory consists of the supplies which you use to make your products. Another part of your inventory consists of the finished product, waiting to be shipped to customers. If you are a retailer, your inventory consists of the finished goods, waiting for customers to order. If you are a service business, your inventory consists of the

employees who come to work every day, waiting for a charge number to put on their time cards so they can work on a paid task. Whenever your employees do not have a charge number for a paid task, they become "overhead." This part of overhead is defined as the people you have to pay to be ready to go when you actually do have work for them. With luck, you can find useful tasks for these employees who are on overhead, such as researching the market and improving your relationships with customers. Of course, you have other, valid overhead expenses, such as marketing and research. Your goal is to keep your labor inventory close to zero, or use it to accomplish valid overhead tasks which you would otherwise have purchased. For example, you might assign employees who are not billing a job to market research projects.

FIFO/LIFO
The best case is to have the lowest possible inventory which does not stop you from making any sales. You have to balance this against the minimum orders required by your suppliers. As you take products out of inventory, your cash register will record the price of the product sold, along with its unique identifying number. You probably are not logging each item individually, but you would log "jar of pickles" as an example, and the number associated with it would tell you the size and supplier of that jar. Your cash register records the number for that jar of pickles, and its price. Deep in the bowels of your accounting software, that special number for that jar of pickles, records your cost for that jar of pickles. But, there's a glitch. You might have bought pickles more than once. Each time you bought them, you might have purchased a whole case. Each case you bought might have been sold to you for a different price. When you sell that jar of pickles for $5, how do you know if it was the jar you bought for $2 or the jar you bought for $2.65? How will you know how much "contribution" that jar of pickles is making to your overhead costs for running the business? Questions like this impact your profit.

If you decide to use the $2 number for your inventory cost

(called "cost of goods sold"), then your pickles offered $3 in contribution ($5 price minus the $2 COGS). If you sold 1,000 of those pickle jars in a month, you might theoretically pay the rent with your gross profit! But if you decide to use the $2.65 for your COGS for pickle jars, then you will theoretically have a lot less money to work with.

Cash is not profit
Now, here's the catch. Neither of those numbers reflects an accurate picture of how much money you have, because the amount of money you have (ie cash) and the amount of profit you are recording on your books, do not mean the same thing. You could use the FIFO method of inventory accounting (FIFO means First In First Out), which would cause you to count the $2 as your COGS. You could use the LIFO method of inventory accounting (Last In First Out), which would cause you to count the $2.65 as your COGS. You could average all your inventory purchases and come up with a number which does not correspond to any number you actually paid. When you were all finished, you could find that you had a profit, which caused you to owe taxes, but you don't have any money in the bank to pay the taxes!

> You could be a highly profitable, broke company, that needed to declare bankruptcy!

Even if you are a service business, the time between contracts causes employees to expect a paycheck, even though there is no work for them to do. You have to keep paying them, because you hope to close another contract soon. If you do, you need the skilled employees available for work on the contract. Inventory is a real dilemma!

Just-in-time inventory
As a smart business owner, you will not buy inventory before you need it. Not even if it's a great deal on sale. Cheap inventory that nobody buys is really expensive. You need a system to plan your purchases. As your company grows, you

need inventory and purchasing software, materials management software, and requirements planning software. As the owner, you need to understand what these software packages do, to be sure you are buying your inventory "just in time" to use it.

Requirements planning software

If your company sells a product, you need a schedule to know when each supply used in manufacturing is running low. You have to know when to reorder, based on the rate at which you are using that material, and the time it takes to receive a new shipment. You have to balance considerations about shelf life of raw materials, quantities needed, rate of use, and time for delivery. Your goal is to order as little as possible, without causing a delay in production or a disruption in sales. If you are selling enough products to support your family, you will find this calculation too complicated to keep in your head. You need more than a spreadsheet to keep these dates and quantities straight.

Requirements planning software lays out a detailed purchasing schedule based on your input. It helps you buy the minimum inventory for your needs. Like all business software, it takes time to learn and use. However, fully automating your processes makes you less dependent on an individual employee and less vulnerable to problems arising from employee turnover.

Key points:
1) *Your inventory needs to be sold, not stored.*
2) *Employees hired for billable tasks can become unjustifiable inventory.*
3) *Averaging inventory can cause you to record costs which reflect no action that ever occurred. This can confuse your decision-making process.*
4) *The best case is to order inventory just in time to use it.*
5) *Requirements planning software can do a great job, if you fully understand its assumptions and models.*

Next lesson: Module 5: Operating, Lesson 4: Customer Relationships

Module 5: Operating
Lesson 4: Customer Relationships

Prompt satisfaction, Good logistics, Informational emails, Review customer profiles, Online communities, Quality assurance

Most of your business will come from repeat customers. Your best advertising will come from them. Your customer focus should revolve around keeping customers happy. It is important to have an actual "relationship" with your customers. They need to feel loyal to your brand, as if buying another brand would be wrong in some way. It's a feeling, a perception, and it can be created through a combination of actions on your part.

Prompt satisfaction
One action you must take is to ensure a quality product, with quick delivery and prompt satisfaction. That is a given, a must-have, a necessity. It is not, however, sufficient, to keep your customers loyal. Loyal customers need to feel a membership in the club: the club of smart and special people who use your brand. Club membership has benefits. The members expect special deals, inside information about new features, maybe even a t-shirt and a baseball cap. Your customers want you to send them emails now and then, but not too often. They want you to inform them of changes and new product introductions. They want to be treated warmly if they call you. They want you to remember their history with your company. They want other people to see them use your product and be impressed with their good judgment.

Good logistics
You need some sort of customer relationship management (CRM) system to be sure your customers are carefully nurtured. You can link your orders, customer service, and daily contacts together, so that any employee of your company can have quick access to the customer history when a call comes in. This way, you won't insult your customers by having them call and talk to

one person and then call back the next day and have to start all over again explaining to a different person.

Informational emails

You need to remind your good customers that you are there for them, waiting for their problem to arise so you can solve it. Emails, but not too many emails, with some information content, can remind them of your solution. If possible, include a special deal, only for them, with every email. Write short articles about the problem for which your product is the solution. Encourage them to stop by the store or order online. Ask them their opinion. Invite them to an in-store event. People need to encounter your product in many ways before they buy. Five or six encounters, through email, ads, or events, are a minimum to break through the consciousness to get a customer to buy.

Review customer profiles

You've profiled your target customer segments. Now that you have actual customers, it would be nice to know if they fit your profiles. If you know your customers, you can talk to them a little, but you can't probe. If, on the other hand, your customers order online, you may never know who they really are. Asking questions of your customers is intrusive, but if you conduct an online blog, you may get to know them just by their voluntary statements. Or, you could start a Facebook fan page and see who shows up! The key is that your customers must consider you reliable, consistent, and trustworthy. If you were a large company, maybe you could get away with some major mistakes. As a small company, however, your reputation is everything. Guard it.

Online communities

Online customer support makes sense in many ways. You can post YouTube videos for training. You can post your Help manual in .pdf format. You can offer live chat forums with customer service managers. You can encourage your customers to discuss your product among themselves in message forums. If you do this, be prepared to participate in those forums and offer quick solutions to customer problems. These forums can serve as testimonials, reviews, investigative analysis, and reassurance that you care about your product. Don't worry too much if you get the occasional detractor on your forums. Every company is susceptible to a chronic detractor on the Internet now and then. For the most part, online consumers know that all reviewers are not created equal. They will look for the consensus, not the outliers. Your support website should be accessible through your website and open to everyone. No password required. Potential buyers will consider your open forums to be thorough and respectful treatment of customers. Consider them part of the purchase analysis.

Quality assurance

Now that customers have access to online reviews, testimonials, support forums, fan pages, and a myriad of possible electronic ways to investigate the opinions of your customers, it is more important than ever to deliver what you promise. You can set up formal procedures for your employees to follow to ensure your products meet quality standards. Simple processes like checklists, two sign-offs on each task, and a final review of the finished product, can all be standard practices in your company culture.

You can also make formal policies for returns. When you sell on the Internet, include a return shipping label with every product. Keep customers, particularly Internet customers, feeling good about their decision to purchase from you. They will tell their friends about their experience. You want that to happen! Word of mouth advertising is your goal! Bend over backwards to accept Internet returns. People will forgive your mistake, but not your rudeness or uncaring behavior.

Key points:
1) *Customer satisfaction drives the conversation on the Internet. You cannot hide, so you must perform.*
2) *CRM software helps your employees keep their contacts straight, both before and after the sale.*
3) *Emails, online support forums, reviews, training videos, and help files are all tools to help you acquire and retain customers.*
4) *Quality products are developed because you check and monitor your processes. What gets measured gets done. What gets rewarded gets repeated.*

Next lesson: Module 5: Operating, Lesson 5: Accounting

Module 5: Operating
Lesson 5: Accounting

Startup cash, The journal entries, Watch your bank balance, Acquisitions, Stock prices

There are many decisions you will make in your business which impact how much your business and you owe in taxes. The purpose of an accountant is to point out the implications of your management options. The accountant can set up your company benefits. This is a very good reason to structure your business as a corporation. Company benefits can cover a wide range of options which enhance your lifestyle. As the CEO, you can decide to offer day care, elder care, health insurance, company cars, expense accounts for corporate entertaining, life insurance, tuition refunds for college, retirement plan matching, and pizza while working overtime. You can stock the corporate refrigerator with unlimited free caffeine drinks. You can install a pool table in the conference room, and depreciate the pool table as a company asset. You can put an Olympic swimming pool in the corporate basement, with a sauna, hot tub, and complete professional gym equipment. You can hold your annual meeting at a beach house. You see, a good accountant is a wonderful addition to your lifestyle. Taxes make a lot of difference in your cash flow, so you need them done very professionally.

Startup cash
Of course, there is that beginning time, when nobody will give you money for your business, and suppliers won't even give you credit. During that time, you probably can avoid paying an accountant. You can start with a spreadsheet on your laptop. On that spreadsheet, you will be concerned not with profit, but with cash flow. If you keep good records of cash flow, you will be able to turn your records over to an accountant later, who will compute the profit and its tax consequences, plus prepare you for future decision-making.

The journal entries

First you will open a spreadsheet called Journal. Get in the habit, every day, of recording every expense. Record the date, how much you paid, who you paid it to, the business purpose of the expense, and the amount. Then file the invoices and cancelled checks by month in folders that match your journal entries. You need to know all these things so that your accountant can categorize it to determine its tax impact. In your Journal, you will also record any receipts the business gets from sales, by date and product line. If you are just starting out, this may not be too onerous to do. As you get employees and real sales, you will also have to do payroll. If you and your spouse are the only employees, you can probably figure it out by using tax software for your pc. The forms that have to be submitted are time-consuming, and well worth a few dollars to have an accounting service do it. If your business is set up as a sole proprietor or a partnership, and you are the only employee, you will not have to pay yourself with a W-2. You will, however, have to submit estimated tax payments which need to be equal for the whole year, thus creating a plethora of dilemmas about how to estimate what, when to estimate it, and how to pay for it with money that hasn't been made yet.

Watch your bank balance

Conserve cash. Lease. Charge. Postpone purchases. Delay payments. Project the need for future bill payments so you can set up a line of credit with your bank to pay them. But above all, do not mess with payroll. If you have employees, pay them on time, and deposit their social security money on time. As a small business manager, cash is your concern. Profit is the concern of your accountant.

Acquisitions

Some companies consider the finance department more important than the operations department. A real estate company might use various accounting rules to obscure losses in one area with acquisitions in another area of the business. Given enough special accounting adjustments, obscurity and your financial statements can be synonyms in the dictionary. It's one thing for your accountant to obfuscate your financials for whatever purpose those actions accomplish. It's another thing altogether for you to be confused by it. Do not allow yourself to be unable to understand your financial statements. Tell your accountant to keep talking until it all makes sense.

Stock prices

Public companies often try to manage their earnings reports to prevent wild fluctuations which alarm the stock market. Be happy, as an entrepreneur, this is not your problem. Your stock doesn't have a real price. You set the price, at whatever you can convince someone to pay for it. In valuing your stock, you focus on solid business principles. You describe a service your business performs for the market. You build a product that delivers on its promises. You let the stock price be the stock price. To help drive this home, search on the Internet and read about the demise of the accounting firm of Arthur Andersen and its client, ENRON. Your business must be about delivery of value. If it is not, you may find yourself feeling ill at the end of your day. Integrity matters.

Key points:
1) *Good accountants are helpful members of your team.*
2) *Pay particular attention to doing payroll correctly and on time.*
3) *It is sometimes possible to obfuscate business financial statements. Just don't obfuscate them from yourself.*
4) *Business is about providing value to customers and delivering on promises. It is not about manipulating stocks. There are other words for stock manipulation.*

Next lesson: Module 5: Operating, Lesson 6: Strategic Relevance

Module 5: Operating
Lesson 6: Strategic Relevance

Strategic options, Tactical moves, Management-by-Walking-Around, Company reward systems

What is business strategy? It is the overall plan to accomplish your mission.   At the top is your mission statement. From the mission statement, you develop a set of goals, and some policies about how you will behave as a company. For example, your company policy may be to only select suppliers who meet certain ethical production standards.   Then you take each goal and come up with a strategy for how to reach it. Suppose your goal is to become the high quality producer of artistically designed but practical walking sticks. You want to dominate the market for these artistic products.   That's the goal. Now how do you go about doing it?   You choose a strategy.   One possible strategy to achieve your goal could be to establish your founder as an expert in hiking, so that his name on the walking stick gives the stick some credibility.

Strategic options
Other possible strategies companies might use to achieve their goals could revolve around pricing, market exposure, branding, and production techniques.   A manufacturing company might choose the strategy to be the low cost producer. It needs this to undercut its competitors' pricing.   Another company might choose to integrate vertically, meaning it controls and owns businesses that make all the various supplies it uses in its products.   Or, a company might choose to integrate horizontally, meaning it owns companies that make a range of products all of the same type. Each of these are strategic decisions, designed to achieve a company's top goal.   One company might choose to keep its costs low by fully automating all its processes and working with a minimal staff.   The strategy a company chooses should support its mission statement.   Of course, no one would choose to spend too much money on operations, but overstaffing

the customer service department could be part of a strategy to respond to customers within five minutes.

Too often, however, small businesses run in a fairly ad hoc manner. The methods and operations evolve, as people respond to unexpected turns of events. The owner doesn't really know what to expect from the market. As a result, he or she is just trying a lot and keeping what works. What works for the current situation may not have been the best or optimal method. It was simply what was available when the emergency arose which caused it to be established. This ability to adapt is essential for a startup business, but equally essential is the insight to step back to review what has occurred.

There is a common saying in business: when you're up to your butt in alligators, it's hard to remember you came here to drain the swamp. That is an excellent description of what happens when an entrepreneur goes to work every day. Small business managers are constantly bombarded with the "dreaded unk unks," the unknown unknowns. You can't anticipate everything that is coming around the corner. As a result, your processes develop tentacles, as if they were some organic material. You have to take a breath, step back, and review what you've done regularly. This is the only way you can see if you are on track to achieve your mission. If you are not, you have to redirect.

Tactical moves

After policy comes strategy. Top management sets policy. Middle management runs operations based on the strategies that implement the policies. First line supervisors monitor the tactical activities which make the strategy work. Suppose it is your company policy to respond to customers within five minutes. Your strategy tells you to staff your customer service department fully. Your tactical operations must include training manuals and practices which teach your customer service employees to be nice to customers and answer quickly. Now suppose your first line supervisors measure customer service employees by how quickly they get the customer off the phone.

Instead of making customers happy with your service, you are angering them by pushing them off the phone. Your tactics do not follow the intent of your strategy. You are sabotaging your mission.

Management-by-Walking-Around

It takes vigilance, and a lot of "management by walking around," to assess whether or not your company's first level tactics are actually relevant to the strategies you have set for your company. A small business manager must walk the floor, listen to the scuttlebutt, and pay attention to the behaviors and reward systems for the employees.

What gets measured gets done. What gets rewarded gets repeated. A small business manager must know what behaviors are getting rewarded in the company. He or she must know this by direct observation, not just by listening to a bunch of "yes people" in a board room. The tactics that are implemented in a company are its de facto strategy, and they lead to achievement of the goals that naturally result from that de facto strategy. The entrepreneur who does not personally see what the company's employees are doing is vulnerable to an unpleasant surprise when the results tally.

Company reward systems

Every year, large company's routinely run through a process called "budgeting." In this process, each department head negotiates up the line for the resources to run the department. By the time the budget process is completed, managers have set their goals for both performance and expenditures. Often, an expectation of compensation is tied to achievement of goals set during this process. Managers work to achieve these goals. If the goals which tie performance to reward are set appropriately, the team works together to achieve them. Working this budget process, many management meetings progress toward consensus. The conflict and contention for limited resources cause the management team to recognize where compromise and retreat may be needed.

In a small company, it is sometimes tempting to avoid the group processes and rule by fiat. Group processes can be excruciatingly slow and annoying. They can feel pointless. They can make you want to grab somebody by the neck and start shaking. Resist the compulsion. When all is said and done, more is said than done, but your managers have achieved "buy-in." The processes help them to agree that the reward is worth the effort. You, as the CEO, are tasked to get their buy-in. Otherwise, you are going to be working night and day, wondering helplessly why nobody can do anything right except you.

Key points:
1) *Top management sets goals, middle management defines the strategy to meet the goals, lower management implements the tactics which manifest the strategy. If the tactics used are not consistent with the goals, you will not reach the goals.*
2) *A disconnect between tactics and strategy can nullify the goals.*
3) *People do what you reward them to do. Incoherent reward systems nullify goals.*
4) *Your management team must agree that the rewards are worth the effort of doing them. Otherwise, they won't do it.*

Next lesson: Module 5: Operating EXERCISES
OR
Module 6: Growing and Exiting, Lesson 1: Managing Cash and Growth

Module 5: Operating
EXERCISES

1. Investigate the options for office space in your area. What are the costs? What options are available for executive suites? Is there a local business incubator in your county? Would it work for your business idea?

2. Write up a staffing plan for your business over time. What would your organization chart look like in two years? In four years?

3. Begin work on your plan of operations. What is your staffing and facilities plan over three years?

Join others to discuss your answers on the AliceElliottBrown.com Business Blog

Module 5: Operating QUIZ

Select True or False for each question.

1. Leasing equipment may be a means to conserve cash and avoid local taxes.

2. Your attorney should attend your marketing meetings.

3. Job descriptions only apply to lower level employees.

4. Small manufacturing companies do not need requirements planning software.

5. It is a good idea to require proof of a defect before accepting customer returns of merchandise bought online.

6. Your stock price, as a private company, reflects an industry standard multiple of earnings.

Check your answers on AliceElliottBrown.com

Module 6: Growing and exiting

6-1: Managing cash and growth
6-2: Developing people
6-3: Monitoring your reputation
6-4: Choosing your successor
6-5: Selling your business
6-6: Living the life you've dreamed

Module 6: Growing and Exiting
Lesson 1: Managing Cash and Growth

Taking more investment, Taking more debt, Increasing margins, Franchising, Staying small

After your business is operating, fast growth means more cash is needed.   You can get cash for growth by taking in more investment, by taking on more debt, or by franchising your operation. More sales do not get you more cash, because the timing of the receipt of money from sales comes later than the cost of producing more product. That means: the faster you grow, the more investment or debt you need. You might show a great profit, which means you owe more taxes, which means you need more cash to pay the taxes, but does not mean you have more cash!   The faster you grow, the worse this cash flow problem becomes. It is a real dilemma.

Taking more investment
When you were looking for help to get your company started, nobody wanted to give you any money for investment. You and just a few friends did this all yourself.   Now it is going well, it has sales, and customers are ordering. You need cash to buy inventory and supplies to fill orders.   Return on investment is practically a sure thing! Now, the investors are ready to give you money.   Now that you've proven the concept, and it's just a matter of delivering and filling orders, they are getting out their checkbooks.   The problem is: they want a big part of your company for doing it.   As more investors come in, your share and the other founders' shares of the company are getting diluted.   You did the real work and took the high risk.   Now others want the reward. It always happens that way. If possible, you will get a good lawyer and structure the offering to the new investors in a way that does not cause you to lose control of the company.   However, finding a competent lawyer who will actually help you is not a given.   You have to learn quite a bit about stock structuring yourself, before you bring in legal

advisors. You have to know what you want and tell them, so they can structure it the way you want it. Good managers do not ask good lawyers to tell them what to do. They decide what they want done and hire the good lawyers to structure it.

You need some cash. If you set up your business as a corporation, you can file some legal paperwork and sell shares in your company directly. You do not have to be selling shares on one of the stock exchanges to sell your stock. You can sell your own shares, as long as you have registered paperwork with the state, and are following that state's rules. Within the constraints set up by the state, you can sell different classes of shares to different potential stockholders. You can have founders' stock, Class A, with different voting rights than the stock you sell later, Class B, or Class C, or Class D through N. As long as you can find someone to buy your shares, you can raise money that way. It is a private offering, not a public one. Study the rules before you do it, and then get a lawyer and an accountant to do what you want done.

Taking more debt

Of course, if you don't want to share the future wealth with more investors, you can try to borrow money to expand. Banks aren't enthusiastic about loaning money for expansion, though. Banks like to loan money for things that can be repossessed. If your expansion includes equipment and facilities, then banks are an option. There is also something called "factoring receivables." This is like taking a payday loan. You get charged an unconscionable price to get somebody else to collect the money your customers owe you. Essentially, you are turning your customers over to a collection agency. This is likely to anger them, which will harm your repeat business.

Increasing margins

Another possible way to get cash for growth is to increase your margins. The "margin" is the difference between a product's price and its variable costs (COGS.) You can get more cash if you have lower overall COGS. With higher margins, you might have enough to reinvest in growth.   There are three methods to increase overall margins.   First, you could introduce a new product line with enhanced features at a higher price. Second, you could review your product offering and discontinue lines with lower margins. Third, you can find cost efficiencies. You should probably plan to do all three of these things anyway, whether they produce the cash you need for growth or not.

Franchising

If you have a successful, profitable, operating business, you might consider franchising it as a means of expansion.   In a franchise operation, you don't own the new facilities. Independent entrepreneurs buy into them. They pay you for the opportunity to use your logo, colors, branding, designs, and overall product concept. You set up a package for them. You tell them which suppliers to use, what products to sell, how to display it, what kind of advertising to use, and whatever other operational procedures work well for your business.   They pay you for the opportunity to use this insight. They must follow certain practices so they will not denigrate your brand. You may also get them to pay you something annually.   This way, your business expands, but you didn't pay for it. The disadvantage of franchising is that it may divert your focus away from operational problems and toward newly-introduced contractual and legal complexities with the franchises. The character of your job may change. You may spend most of your time dealing with contract disputes instead of running the company.

Staying small

Those are the only options you have. If you want to grow, you put more money in.   You can put it in through investment, through debt, through increasing margins, or through selling off your brand in a franchising deal.   If none of those options sound attractive, why not stay small and just make a living for your family? There are arguments for staying small. You do not have to grow or die. You do have to wake up happy in the morning, excited to begin your day. If growth induces the stress which impedes your happiness, why grow?

Key points:
1) *Growth requires cash.*
2) *Cash usually comes from debt or investment.*
3) *Franchising may offer a way to grow.*
4) *Protecting and refreshing your margins are good ideas under any circumstance.*
5) *Growth is not the goal. Happiness is the goal.*

Next Lesson: Module 6: Growing and Exiting, Lesson 2: Developing People

Module 6: Growing and Exiting
Lesson 2: Developing People

What motivates people, Perceptions of value, Expectations of reward, Self-esteem, De-motivators, Steps to motivate, Agony of the chief

One of the biggest mistakes new managers and new entrepreneurs make is feeling they have to do everything themselves. Nobody else does it right. *If you want it done right, you have to do it yourself. You just can't get good help any more.* It's true that other people can't read your mind; they may not do it the way you would do it. You must step back and let them do things their way, after you tell them what result you want. People don't all get to the same point by the same path. Once you explain where the point is, you have to let them find their own way to get there.

What motivates people?

The question of what causes people to work harder is one which comes up in every business. This is a topic which has been studied extensively in management research, and it has an answer.

The answer is:

> *People will work harder when the Expected Reward, multiplied by the Person's Assigned Value to that reward, and divided by the Person's Expectation of Receiving that reward is a positive number.*

What does that mean? Let's say the reward offered is more money. This is a classic, because study after study proves that money is not a motivator. Lack of money is a de-motivator, but money quickly adapts to become an expectation. If you take money away, you de-motivate, but if you add money, you don't get anybody to work harder for it. Actions that are perceived as punishing de-motivate and cause passive-aggressive responses. Actions that are perceived as rewarding motivate if and only if they are randomly applied. That is, any regularly applied reward, on a schedule with a clear set of rules, passes from the category of "reward" to the category of "expectation." To remove or withhold the expectation then becomes a punishment. The reward loses its effectiveness as a motivator, because it is perceived to be the consequence of continuing to work in accordance with the status quo. The inexperienced manager easily falls into the trap of wondering why the clear rewards offered are not causing any results.

> *Think of it this way: suppose that every Wednesday, you go to lunch at a Persian restaurant. You love it. You look forward to your Wednesday trip. After a while, it becomes a punishment to not be able to go to the restaurant on Wednesday, instead of a reward to go. You come to expect that this activity is part of the "daily life as usual", rather than a treat. The trip to the restaurant loses its motivating value, but the loss of the trip to the restaurant makes you feel depressed.*

What you're trying to do in motivating people to work harder is to first keep them from feeling depressed and sabotaging the company. If you can accomplish that feat, then the next question is: how can you get more out of them?

Perception of value
The first rule in motivating people is:

1. Any benefit, salary, bonus, or expectation, once given, can never be taken away. You will cause such a flood of negative emotion that you will find yourself wondering why your employees hate you. This emotion will not be admitted or expressed. It will just be manifested as passively aggressive sabotage. This is why you don't write an operations manual that tells people *what* they can expect and *when* they can expect it. Those expectations have a big downside, and don't cause the desired behavior.

Every person has their own "currency of value", or things which they are willing to work for. That currency, counter-intuitively, is never money. If money solved anything, then when people who are making money reached a level of enough, they would stop trying to make it. You wouldn't see people who get $98M bonuses, because there isn't all that much one can buy in a life that would allow that much money to be spent. Rather, people are motivated by approval, feelings of competence, feelings of self-worth, and a search for meaning. The $98M bonus is a measuring stick for that person's self-worth. If he didn't get it, he might feel depression. Their personal identity is tied to the money.

People want their "attaboys". They will work for them. The manager who sincerely notices the good things about people will get loyal employees, willing to go the extra mile. *If you point out what is right, instead of what is wrong, you will learn that what gets rewarded gets repeated.* The good behavior, and the high performers, are those with whom a manager should spend his time and effort. "Attention of the manager" is considered highly rewarding by people. People will do what they see causes that attention. The manager who gives his attention to the poor performers, will get more poor performance.

Expectation of reward
The second rule of motivating people is then:
2. Ignore bad behavior. Pay attention to good behavior, because that is what you want repeated.

> *Example: Suppose you have a problem in getting people to turn off the lights and lock the door when they leave. Rather than harp on "who forgot to lock the door", what you do is harp on "who remembered to lock the door". Positively. Others, noticing that locking the door gets your attention, then remember to lock the door, because they are not passively-aggressively blocking you for harping on them. Always remember this: your attention is the reward. When someone gets your attention, they will repeat that behavior. If you only pay attention to negative*

*behavior, your employees will give you more of it. It works
the same way that it works with your children.*

We've covered the Expected Reward and the employee's currency of value. Telling someone they will receive a $100 a month raise if they do a specific set of tasks may not motivate them because they will weigh the cost of doing the tasks against the value of a $100 raise. They may say "I will have a better life if I do not put out the effort to do those tasks, because that is too much effort just for a $100 raise." People strongly search for equity in their work. They will assess and measure the other employees against their personal standard. They judge whether they are working harder than their colleagues. If they believe they are working harder than others, they will reduce their effort in order to attain equity. In addition to assessing this balance between equity and value currency, the third criteria that an employee takes into account when deciding how hard they will work is "expectation of receiving the reward."

Tip: Suppose you tell your employees they will all get a small ownership in the company through an employee stock ownership plan. The value of that ownership depends on the company growing. Employees will assess whether or not they think the growth will occur. They won't work like dogs to make the company grow, because they believe growth of the company is not a function of their personal work. And it isn't. It is a function of the work of the top dogs, not the employees. We all know what the scenery is if you're not the top dog. As a result, ESOP plans are seldom motivators for non-executive employees.

Self-esteem
The third rule of motivating people is then:
3. You must offer something that the person both wants and also believes is attainable through his own effort. What the person wants is self-esteem and a sense of meaningfulness. Titles, offices, expense accounts, days off, privileges, and chits you post on your door to show your achievements, are all motivators, as

long as they are perceived to be attainable.

> *Here is an example of a motivator that meets the criteria. Let's say you tell your employees they will get a little icon-medal to hang on their office door each time they work on a project. The medals show others in the company that you were a team member on that project. People with the most projects can show others in the company how valuable they are. This makes people happy. They clamor to get on a team, just so they could hang the little medal on their door. Why?*

Because the Expected Reward (the little icon-medal) has a Perceived Value (status in the eyes of their colleagues). Everybody on the team receives the medal, with no differentiation of how much effort they put in. Therefore, the cost of attaining this reward is low. All you had to do was be on the team, even if you didn't do much. The Expectation of Receiving the Reward was high, because there was no qualifying hoop to jump through. Just be on the team. As a result, it motivated people to want to be on a team. Once they were on the team, the comradery of the group motivated them to put forth a good effort. This was an excellent example of a motivator.

De-motivators
Here are some de-motivators:

> - tell somebody they have been promoted, and then ask them to do something they have no background or experience to know how to do, leaving them with a feeling of incompetence. Then threaten to take the promotion away, or worse.

> - at a time when the company is dealing with increased customer problems, due to product immaturity, ask the employees to add to their workload after hours in preparation for anticipated growth

- in the stage of a company where you have only five employees, and every person needs to step in and be willing to do anything at any time, put structure in place that implies that there are specific job duties for specific people. This will cause employees to stop doing what is not on their list.

Companies have stages of maturity. In the startup phase, which continues until you have at least 40 employees, you need a sense of comradery and team spirit that will allow everyone to help everyone else with whatever needs to be done. This comradery is dampened or discouraged by senses of inequality. People seek equity and they work to see themselves as a valuable person on the team. Titles and hierarchy squelch that team effort. On the other hand, you have to set ground rules and expectations for what has to get done. It's a balancing act. You need job descriptions, but you need some level of vagueness and imprecision in them. It's not going to be a formula, whereby you do x, y, and z and then you get promoted. In the life cycle of the company, you are ultimately going to need 90% of your employees to be Indians, not Chiefs. That means until you have 20 employees, you aren't going to run into or need another Chief, beyond the company president.

Chiefs aren't created by personnel policies. They arrive and announce themselves to you. You find them in the recruiting and hiring process, not the personnel development process. In asking the question: how do I develop my in-house management for growth, the answer is: you hire correctly. Leaders are born, not made. You can teach leadership, but you have to be working with talented raw material. While you certainly can do much to develop your managers, you aren't going to turn them into leaders unless they arrived that way when you met them. The standard answer when Harvard Business School was asked how they get such a high percentage of successful graduates is: "We look for applicants who are going to succeed anyway, and we rush in and stamp Harvard on their foreheads." As a manager, your employees great successes are not your fault.

Each person who is your employee wants to go home at night feeling good about themselves. You don't need them each to be obsessive, each to want to give their all to the company and work 80 hour workweeks. Only a very few will ever do that, and it will never be your decision which ones make that choice. Those who do will be doing it for something inside of them, not through any action you take to motivate them. When you run into one of these people, in the hiring process, you may find that you are not ready for them, and you may pass on the hire. These people often run their own companies because no one will hire them.

Steps to motivate
So, we are left with the question: how do you motivate employees? We've talked a lot about what does not motivate. Here is the simple answer:

1. You clearly and specifically express what you want.

2. You notice and reward with attention and positive feedback when you get what you asked for.

3. You praise and encourage activities that are above and beyond what you asked for.

4. You nurture team spirit by offering group rewards on a random and occasional basis (remember rewards cannot be regular or expected.)

5. You pay attention to equitable and fair treatment of everyone, knowing that people look for equity.

6. You accept your employees for what they offer, not for what they lack.

Agreed, there are different rules for that 10% who fall into the Chiefs category. But 90% of your employees don't. You don't want them to. Too many cooks spoil the stew. Too many chiefs, not enough Indians. Whatever anomaly of obsession makes a person chase the unbalanced life of raw ambition, you can't force it. Let it be.

Agony of the chief

In the end, the fish stinks from the head down. Your employees want to come to work, make a meaningful contribution, feel good about what they did, and go home. That's another one of those facts of life. It just is what it is. Accept that, and take what they have to offer. Giving people grief does not motivate them. You are the person who makes the big bucks and expects the big reward. They are not. The only person who deserves to agonize over this business is *you*.

Key points:
1) *People work harder when they believe they will get something for their effort.*
2) *Money is not a motivator, but lack of money is de-motivator.*
3) *Every person has their own currency of value.*
4) *Spend your management time with the high performers.*
5) *People want self-esteem and meaning from their work.*
6) *The fish stinks from the head down. The responsibility for the health of the working environment lies with you.*

Next lesson: Module 6: Growing and Exiting, Lesson 3: Monitoring your reputation

Module 6: Growing and Exiting
Lesson 3: Monitoring your reputation

Negative publicity, Libel and slander, Show your sensitivity

Google yourself regularly. Your online reputation, in today's world, is your effective reputation. Negative stories about you, posted on blogs, Facebook, message boards, or individual websites, do have the power to seriously harm your business. Positive messages in these same places are your hope for fast growth, and you want positive messages. While you want positive messages, you cannot avoid negative ones. Every company will get some Internet detractors now and then.

Negative publicity
What should you do if someone posts negative messages about your company on the Internet? What you should *not* do is post a denial and link to the negative message. A company named Fibrowatt did exactly that. Some very negative websites were set up to give unflattering information about their company. On the company Blog, Fibrowatt issued a denial and linked to the negative sites. It might be one argument to address the questions head on, but addressing and answering the questions is a vastly different activity from linking to the negative website. First, you are increasing traffic to the negative website. Second, you sound like you are whining and making excuses. A better response is to select the negative questions and give honest, straightforward answers without identifying the source of the questions.

Libel and slander
If the information posted about you is opinion, there is not much you can do about it. Opinions are what they are. If, however, someone is posting untrue statements about you or your company, that is called "libel," and it is something for which your lawyer can take action. Libel is defined as written lies, while slander is defined as verbal lies. Often just being contacted by an attorney will be enough to get the offending information

removed. You can also contact the ISP and ask for the information to be removed, if you say it is untrue. Untrue information may have been posted by a disgruntled ex-employee, or even ex-business partner. It could have been posted by an anonymous commenter on a Blog. You can pursue that with threats of court action.

Show your sensitivity
Your problem arises only when the information is true. If it is true, you should thank the person who told you. Clearly, you didn't know, or you would never have run your business that way. Immediately make changes, and post about the changes on your own website. Turn the lemons into lemonade, and publicize the new you.

You also can set up some new blogs of your own, and write positive things about how you made these changes. If possible, fill up the first search page on Google with new websites that all link to each other and all talk about the improvements you've made.

Key points:
    1) You can't control what is written about you on the Internet.
    2) You can protect yourself from libel.
    3) You can participate and make your case online.

Next Lesson: Module 6: Growing and Exiting, Lesson 4: Choosing your successor

Module 6: Growing and Exiting
Lesson 4: Choosing your successor

The family business, Selecting a leader, Informal authority

There was a time when it was assumed your successor would be your first-born son, like an inherited monarchy.   As business became globally competitive, it became clear that one cannot really inherit a business if the talent and desire are not there.   As we saw sons inherit their father's businesses, we were reminded of the old adage:
Question: How do you make a small fortune?
Answer: Start with a big fortune.

We realized that running a business takes both education and talent.   Once you have managed your business to success, you will immediately begin grooming your successor. Why? Because what is the point of working so hard if you never have time to enjoy your life?   You cannot be the only person capable of running this business.   Somebody has to be capable of pinch hitting for you. What if you get an opportunity to take the kids on an African safari for a month?   Do you have to pass on the chance because the business can't operate without you?   Your life will be far more enjoyable if you have a second-in-command who is fully capable.

The family business
What about preparing your children to take over? If you are running an attractive small business, without partners, and its purpose is to provide a lifestyle for your family for generations, then you will definitely want your children to take over.   But, is that what your children want? Many entrepreneurs have set up the business for their children and learned too late that their children didn't care.   It is disheartening to make decisions with the next three generations in mind, only to learn that your children would join the circus before they would take over for you.

In the other direction, some entrepreneurs have found that setting up their children to compete for control of the family business creates a highly dysfunctional family. We say there are things money cannot buy. One thing money can buy? Family conflict, when money becomes a measure of personal value and position in the family relationship. Your children would be better off if you gave your money to charity, than they will be if you set them against each other for control of the company. Your best bet is to write a will that gives each of your children an equal share, and let the company choose the best qualified person to be CEO through well-thought-out human relations processes. If one of your children chooses to compete in that process, that is your child's decision, not yours. Your child may indeed be the best qualified person for the job. Let the management team make that decision, just as they would if you had no children.

> Question: Do you know who is President of the Teamsters Union in the year 2010?
> Answer: Jimmy Hoffa, Jr. has been elected four times
> The Teamsters Union is a business itself. Its President is elected by the union members. Jimmy Hoffa was certainly its most famous leader. He disappeared in 1975. The members elected his son President four times in a row.

If one of your children is the right person to run your business, trust that the process you put in place to select a President will make the right choice.

Selecting a leader.

There are two processes. The formal process to select your replacement is one which you should write in your company Bylaws. This will institutionalize the process, and prevent the sort of "palace coup" we read about in history books of the monarchies. By the time your business is large enough to be concerned about succession, you will have a Board of Directors, a management team, and legal advisors. Bylaws should have a section which spells out what will happen when you step down. Because it may be out of your control at that time, it may not happen as you foresee it. Others will participate in that decision. This is right, because once your company succeeds, others depend on it. Others have a stake in the company. Others have a need and a right to participate in the decision-making. It is no longer just about *you. It may be hard to accept, but others helped you make this company successful, and others can carry the burden without you.* Don't make them pry your cold, dead fingers off the controls. Plan to give it up and retire.

The informal authority
Informally, you will notice which of your managers, or your children, shows an interest and a proclivity to do well at running the business. Trying not to be obvious about it, you will slowly arrange for that person to have opportunities to learn, with some measure of protection against failure. Over time, you will talk to them, teach them, coach them, and encourage them. You will step back and allow them to try things on their own. You will remember that we don't learn from success, we learn from failure. You will let them know you trust their judgment and support their dreams. Maybe they will rise to the occasion. Maybe they will not. That will be their decision. Your choice will be to offer the opportunities to learn, and the encouragement to dream. After that, it is out of your hands.

Not everything is within your control. You don't want it to be. You fulfilled your dream with this business. You took it to a certain point, where you will turn it over to someone else. Then, you will leave.
Key points:
1) *Your children may not want to take over.*
2) *You need a management team and a set of formal succession procedures.*
3) *Informal processes give opportunity and encouragement.*
4) *We learn from failure.*

Next lesson: Module 6: Growing and Exiting, Lesson 5: Selling your business

Module 6: Growing and Exiting
Lesson 5: Selling your business

How to calculate value, The price is personal

You've realized your dreams, your business is successful, and you want to cash out. Why do you want to cash out? Because that was the goal from day one. What? You thought you did this because you wanted to provide sequined handbags to every person in the world, and that was your dream?   Of course not. You did want to provide those handbags, but above all else, you did this to support your family, and now you want it to support your retirement. You may even want to retire at an early age, so you want the best possible sale price for this company you built.

How to calculate value
The value of your company is whatever you can convince someone to pay for it. This buyer is probably not going to come looking for you. You will have to put together a sales package and look for the buyer. Your company has the following tangible arguments which support its price:
1.   The value of future cash flows
2.   The value of current assets

> You have a profitable business at this point.   If your business is still unprofitable, selling it is one of those matters of luck and fate. If you have a profitable business, you can ask for some multiple of earnings as your selling price.

> *If you were a public company, other companies in your industry which are public companies sell their stock for a certain price per share. This price is X times the company's earnings per share.   This is called the P/E ratio.   Price divided by Earnings. In your industry, companies might be selling for 9 times earnings.   You can set your asking price at 9 times your annual earnings. This can be the start of a negotiation.   Your buyer, of course, will reject that*

argument and make a counter-argument. In the end, you sell for a number which will meet your objectives for retirement, and be happy with that.

The price is personal

You will need that good accountant and competent attorney to help you negotiate. You might offer to sell the business to your current management team. You might take your payment over time, as a percentage of future revenue. What will actually happen is that you will figure out how much money you need to live a good life and retire happily, and anything above that is pure gravy. There is no objective number for how much your company is worth. You will put forth arguments about the value of your brand name, your good will in the community, your customer base, your projected future cash flows, and the worth of your inventory. They are all just arguments. Depending on the goals and objectives of the potential buyer, they will carry more or less weight. You will sell your company for a number that will allow you to live happily for the rest of your life. If no one will pay you the number you want, don't sell. Keep running your business. After all, it's a good life, isn't it?

Key points:

1) *Your business value is based on the perception of future cash flows as well as current assets.*
2) *You may be its only real value. It may be worth less to others than it is to you.*
3) *If running your business does not make you happy, why are you doing it? Stop! Take what you can get and move on.*
4) *If running your business does make you happy, why sell it?*

Next lesson: Module 6: Growing and Exiting, Lesson 6: Living the life you've dreamed

Module 6: Growing and Exiting
Lesson 6: Living the Life You've Dreamed

Waiting to retire, Live every day in the here and the now, The business must be the vision, Every day is a good day

You did it. You started your business. You ran it. You sold it. You retired. Now it's time to . . .

> *Wait a minute. You waited until you retired to start living the life of your dreams? What are you? Age sixty? Sixty-six?*

Too many of us drag ourselves through life, getting through it. Passing time. Spending time. Wasting time. Killing time. Playing application games on Facebook. Posting on MySpace. Dibbling and dabbling. Piddling. Getting wasted. Partying.

Waiting to retire

We're waiting. Waiting until we retire so we can start living. Waiting to save up enough money to go to Barbados. We wait for the music to start, so we'll know it's time to start living. We imagine we need more money. We think all will be well, when we meet the next goal, lose twenty pounds, save the magic number, or get the kids through college. We live waiting for the future. The present, we find numbing. The past, we find traumatic. So we wait to live. We try not to think, because our thoughts disturb us.

It takes a lot out of a person, to run their own business. Superhuman effort. Endless hours. Nearly unbearable uncertainty, anxiety, and stress. A lot of *ups*. A lot of *downs*. A lot of disappointments. A lot of exhilarations. In the end, a satisfaction that you did it. You provided jobs for others. You supported your family. You contributed to the economy. You paid taxes. You greased the wheels of commerce so the wealth could trickle down. You're pleased and happy with what you've done.

Live everyday in the here and the now
You must also be happy with how you lived each day. As you ran your business, as you developed your employees, as you built your customer base, you also had to live your dream. You had to feel that each action you took, you took in concert with your own integrity. You had to believe that you lived up to your own value system. Every day, you had to feel pleased with how you were living. That is why you had to choose a business you enjoyed.

The stresses of your business must invigorate you. The challenges must empower you. The low points must motivate you. The high points must nourish your soul. You must be living the life you've dreamed *while* you are running your business.

The business must be the vision
It doesn't work to hang around dreaming of the day you get rich from your business so you can quit doing it and go live your dream. *The only way you can be a successful entrepreneur is if the business **is** your dream.* If you have no such dream, your foray into the business world could be torture.

These are the advantages of running your own business:
> You control how you spend your day.
> You decide what you will do.
> You live with the consequences of your decisions.

These are the disadvantages of running your own business:
> You control how you spend your day.
> You decide what you will do.
> You live with the consequences of your decisions.

Sometimes, a person will think they want to run their own business, when what they really want is to win the lottery. They just want to get rich. You might get rich running your own business. It could happen. That might be a consequence. But, then again, you could also get poor. Your question, before you decide to start your own business is: *Am I ready to be responsible for my own fate? Can I live with what happens next, without imposing a right or a wrong on it? Am I able to deal with failure as a learning experience, without incorporating it into my identity? Can I avoid seeing myself as a dumb klutz, every time something goes wrong? Can I keep an objective outlook, so that I can learn from every problem, and re-direct my goal? Can I understand that I do not control the universe, so I can pay attention and respond to it? Can I look at the world and accept how it behaves?*

The successful entrepreneur sees a bandwagon and rides it. He doesn't build it. He notices it. He may have been the first to notice it, but he doesn't fool himself into thinking he created it. He goes with the market. He serves the market need. Arrogance is not a characteristic of a great leader. The leader always serves.

Every day is a good day
To run your business successfully, the life you live while running it must be the life of your dreams. When you reach the age of retirement, you say good-bye and move on, to a new dream, a new goal. Maybe, even, a new business.

Key points:
   1) *Living the life of your dreams is not something you put off for retirement.*
   2) *Your business must be enjoyable day by day.*
   3) *You must live in the present, the here and the now.*

Next lesson: Module 6: Growing and Exiting EXERCISES

Module 6: Growing and Exiting
EXERCISES

1. Learn about Maslow's Hierarchy of Needs by searching the Internet.   What can you apply from this theory in your own management style?

2. Search the Internet for information about how to do an Initial Public Offering on the Vancouver Stock Exchange. What is involved?

3. Complete your business plan based on everything you have learned. Follow the outline given in Module 1: Planning, Lesson 6: Writing the Business Plan

Join others to discuss your answers on the AliceElliottBrown.com Business Blog

Module 6: Growing and Exiting QUIZ

1. Selling the rights to your name, logo, branding, and business practices is called
   a. Trade rights
   b. Franchising
   c. Acquisition
   d. Merger

2. The options for growing your business require:
   a. Cash
   b. Solid ideas
   c. Good management
   d. High inventory

3. People will work harder if
   a. You pay them more
   b. You promote them
   c. Their team is winning
   d. They believe they will get something they value

4. The goal of your personnel policies should be to:
   a. Make leaders of every person
   b. Prevent employee sabotage
   c. Get everyone to do their personal best
   d. Reward and punish appropriately

5. There is nothing you can do to prevent:
   a. Customer dissatisfaction
   b. Employee sabotage
   c. Lies about you from being posted on the Internet
   d. Negative opinions about you from being posted on the Internet

6. The means of choosing the next president of your company should be written in your corporate:
   a. Bylaws
   b. Articles of incorporation

c. Personnel policies
d. Business plan

*Check your answers on
AliceElliottBrown.com*

Module 7: Getting a Life

The conclusion.

"I have a cow. You have a bull. Let's make a deal."

That is the basis of business. Business is an agreed transaction between cooperating parties. Too often, inexperienced managers ask their lawyers to make a deal. Or, they simply agree to the terms offered by the opposing party. Too often, one party feels disadvantaged, seceding power to the other party. In a good business deal, both parties win.

We are fortunate, as citizens of the United States of America, to live in a nation where you may offer your work in return for another person's money. If you can find a buyer for your services, you are free to sell them. You can get a license to do business at your local county courthouse. There is a low fee, and there are a few innocuous questions. You need not justify your desire, or explain your business. The only requirement is to perform services that are lawful, and agree to file and pay your taxes. You do not need an attorney to obtain your business license. You only need a valid address and a list of the owners and directors.

This right, to do lawful business freely, is an unparalleled competitive advantage for the United States in a global marketplace.

Think back to the Thirteen Colonies in the New World. What was happening? A territory full of abundant natural resources developed. People needed houses, food, heat, lighting, furniture, entertainment, and rules for living. They were separated from the civilized world of Europe, by an arduous journey by ship. To survive, they had to develop skills, which their neighbors would pay to obtain. One became the butcher. One became the baker. One became the shoemaker, the candlestick maker, the firewood hauler, and the weaver. The economy developed village by village. Over time, all the services required for a comfortable life appeared. Neighbors, one by one, chose their calling. They did not live in isolation, independently. They lived in villages, and each person chose a service to provide. Somebody had to shoe the horses, build the wagons, and forge the tools. The economy was primarily a local economy, with local food from nearby farms.

Sometimes we forget that this local economy developed over a period of nearly two hundred years before the Revolutionary War. The states existed as colonies for nearly as long as the nation has existed independently. During this time, local craftsmen offered their wares to willing buyers. Those who got sick depended on doctors who made their own decisions about the ability of their patients to pay. The doctor served the community. One cannot envision the local response if a doctor refused to care for someone in the community because they could not pay.

As the economy grew, some businesses got bigger. Before long, wages in Baltimore fell below wages in Boston. Companies started preferring to hire in Baltimore. In response, craft guilds formed. These were groups of professional craftsmen, who joined together to fight the trend of sending work to Baltimore for the lower prices. It was like outsourcing, for the colonies. Baltimore was the Mexico of the 1700's.

The craft guilds set standards, and hired apprentices to learn the trades. Their goal was to establish professionalism among others in the same industry. By the 1800's, local craftsmen began to be replaced by assembly-line manufacturing. There was great concern that working on an assembly line would de-humanize people. A shoemaker once took pride in making each pair of shoes unique. Now, making the shoes all alike was a goal. No person could say they made a pair of shoes any more. Now, they made only the laces, or only the soles, or only the heels. They were cogs in a machine, just parts of the assembly line.

By 1869, a group of tailors decided to do something about the encroachment of machinery, which took away the human soul. They founded the Noble and Holy Order of the Knights of Labor. The Knights of Labor called for an end to child labor and championed the eight-hour workday. Somehow or another, this resulted in riots in Chicago. In the process of a peaceful protest over a police action that had injured and killed striking workers, a bomb somehow got thrown toward a policeman. This caused the policemen to fire into the crowd, killing peaceful protestors.

Nationwide hysteria, which followed this riot, effectively ended the Knights of Labor. The eight-hour workday got lost in the process.

From the ashes of the Knights of Labor rose two phoenix. One was named the International Workers of the World. This group advocated an end to capitalism. These are the "commies" whom we associate with the beginnings of labor unions. They wanted a socialist structure. This group did not catch on, among the early Americans, and does not survive as a strong group today.

The second group was the American Federation of Labor. The A F of L was strongly pro-capitalist, then, as it is now. Their leadership wanted to strengthen business, improve its productivity, and enhance its profitability. Their only request was that the workers, who participated in the team that caused this success, receive their just and equitable piece of the pie. They wanted to negotiate with company management, in order to balance the power between workers and owners. More importantly, the A F of L was not a super-union. It was a federation, or association, of many local unions. The local unions would make their own rules. The federation would be there for advice and counsel.

The strength of American manufacturing increased, and with it, the labor unions grew. Americans built a solid middle class. Factory workers earned enough to send their children to college. Workers could expect to receive health care, retirement benefits, sick pay, and vacations. One could plan to work an entire lifetime for one company. Each generation came to expect to achieve a higher standard of living than their parents before them. We laughed at labels that read: "made in Japan." America had the technology. America had the manufacturing. American-made was the quality label. Our families lived comfortably on one income. Women stayed in the home. The middle class thrived and grew.

Then something evil this way came.
Whatever it was, we lost our manufacturing. Our factories closed. Our banks took over, as the drivers of our economy. We became a nation of "service" jobs. We became an "information" economy. We stopped making things and selling them to our neighbors.

Companies started charging employees for their health insurance. Benefit plans limited our number of sick days. Doctors lost control of whom they would treat for free. Families could no longer survive on one income. Company retirees discovered their retirement plans had switched from a "defined benefit" to a "defined contribution." We no longer knew how much we would make when we retired, based on a company-paid contribution. We only knew how much would be taken out of our paychecks to invest our own money for our retirement. All risk moved from the company to the employee. The labor unions dropped in membership until they became nearly irrelevant.

Then, in 2008, we learned the phrase "too big to fail." Our government reached in to "save" our banks. Our banks responded by distributing the taxpayer's money as bonuses to their managers.

American capitalism was essentially dead.

I still have a cow. You still have a bull. We can still make a deal.

But fortunately, with the closed door to formal capitalism, came the open window for the beleaguered middle class. The Internet broke the barriers to global competition. Because the Internet allows access to customers, with little cost to reach them, I can still trade with you, worldwide.

I don't need no govm't intervention. I got a cow. You got a bull. We can make a deal.

Business is *that* simple. A capable seller finds a willing buyer. The rest is administrivia.

As the use of the Internet transforms industries, musicians, artists, craftsmen, engineers, inventors, developers, film makers, and authors are able to reach their potential customers directly, in the form of the global village. Business can find, inform, offer, and distribute its products globally, in ways that were never before possible. The barriers to offering service and finding the right customer are crumbling. As more people realize that business is no more than the mechanics of making a good deal for yourself and your customer, the power of the Internet enables the creative and ambitious forces within all of us. We awake to our power.

Getting a Life; Making a Living is a handbook. A reference guide to be consulted as you need it. I hope it gets you started. I hope it erases the fear of the unknown. If you choose to start your own business, remember this thought from Henry David Thoreau:

If we walk confidently in the direction of our dreams, and endeavor to live the life which we have imagined, we experience a success unexpected in common hours.

. . . Thoreau

The Master Of My Universe Series

Books by Alice Elliott Brown

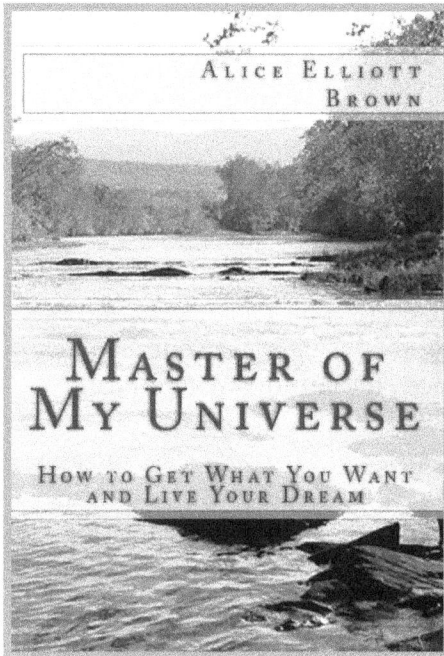

Book One:

Master of My Universe

How to get what you want and live your dream

If you need help sorting out your everyday conflicts and demands, *Master of My Universe* is your step-by-step guide to winning at life. From work stresses, to health problems, to family conflict, this book shows you how to get what you want and live your dream. In this book, you will learn: how to find out what success means to you, how to transform your vision into a plan, and how to make your plan become your reality.

Master of My Universe challenges you to live your dream.

Written with great humor and wisdom by an author with an active, fertile mind, honed by the study of many disciplines, Master of My Universe author Elliott-Brown charms us out of traditional modes of thinking in order to undertake the most important, joy-inducing journey of our lives - to determine our heart's desire. And then, much to our surprise, she shows us how to achieve it.

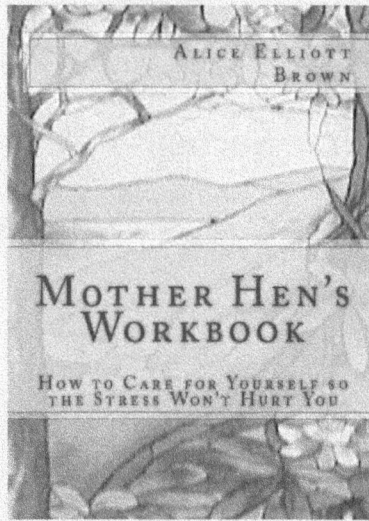

Book Two:

Mother Hen's Workbook

How to care for yourself

so the stress won't hurt you

Caring for ourselves involves life management in multiple dimensions. *Mother Hen's Workbook* provides the forms, charts, measurement systems, and feedback you need to structure a healing therapy program for yourself. Covering eight forms of therapy, Elliott-Brown helps you get in touch with all aspects of yourself to calm your nerves and relieve the stresses of living. This book ties the aspects of the inner mind into a set of therapeutic practices for improving your health and your life.

As a companion book to Brown's *Master of My Universe: How to get what you want and live your dream,* this book gets you past the stage of "chosen illness" so you can live the best life possible for you. We each have a "best life possible." While every illness is not caused by stress, many of our symptoms can be relieved when the stresses in our lives are released. *Mother Hen's Workbook* offers the structure to unburden our stresses and become the best that we each have inside.

If you have a niggling little voice inside, begging for relief, *Mother Hen's Workbook* can help you release the baggage you carry and start over with a fresh new day.

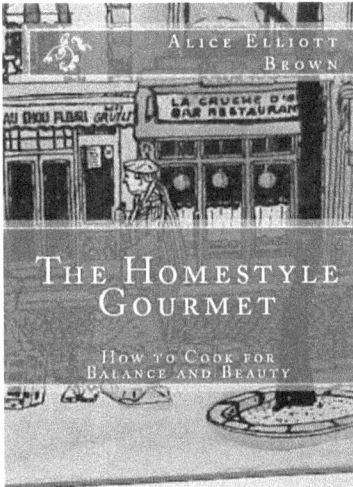

Book Three:

The Homestyle Gourmet

How to cook for

balance and beauty

There are two ways to stop a pot of water from boiling, Brown tells us. We can inject the water with chemicals to raise its boiling point, or we can turn off the heat. This engaging cookbook explains why our Standard American Diet is the equivalent of raising the boiling point on our health. Filled with recipes for healthy, whole foods, Brown writes for the home cook, with commonly available ingredients, simple cooking methods, and a sustainable pantry.

If you suffer from vague, chronic symptoms, wonder why you don't always feel your best, and want to improve your family's health, cooking everything "from scratch," and eating fresh from the farm, is your best chance. Cooking whole, natural foods is a tactic toward your goal to live a long and healthy life. Happily, when you cook, the rest of your family gets to eat the food, too. They get to smell the simmering aromas and the baking cinnamon and vanilla. They get to live in the house with the happy cooking smells. They get to improve their health, enhance their attitude, and increase their energy. So if your *Master of My Universe* goal included "improving your family life," cooking whole, natural foods is a bonus tactic to meet that goal.

Alice Elliott Brown shows you how to cook and be healthy within the constraints of an active life. *And, of course, it's gluten-free.*

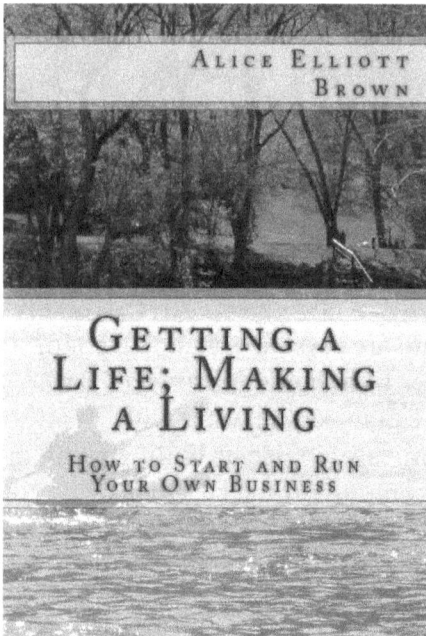

Book Four:

Getting a Life; Making a Living

How to start and run your own business

It can be hard to master your universe if your time is committed to a job you hate. Making your own path in life still requires a steady paycheck. *Getting a Life; Making a Living* offers the first-time entrepreneur a simple course in practical business. Covering topics from registering your business at the county courthouse to finding your target customers, Brown guides you to success. If you are wondering what to do to meet your career goals, *Getting a Life; Making a Living* shows you how to navigate the waters to sail your own ship. Structured as an introductory training course, this book gets you started on your own path.

The course describes how to plan, fund, structure, market, operate, grow, and exit your small business. Because how can we pursue happiness, if we spend our time, which is our life, doing a job that we hate?

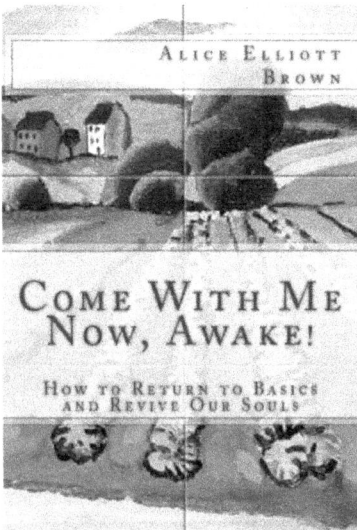

Book Five:

Come With Me Now, Awake!

How to return to basics and revive our souls

Have you ever wanted to give it all up and run away? Are you feeling trapped by a job, by a paycheck, or by a neighborhood? Do you worry about what will happen when the debt ceiling stops rising, inflation eats your savings, and the Big Bad Terrorists collapse the electric grid? Returning to the land, to the basics, and to the soul of our society is becoming a lost art. More and more people lose themselves in the six inch screens of their smartphones: texting, updating their Facebook pages, and losing the intimate connection with others that comes from face-to-face, in-person relationships.

In *Come With Me Now, Awake!,* Brown gives us the How-to on returning to invigorating, aware living, so you and your family can live self-sufficiently. Covering food storage, water filtering, energy generation, sustainability, and the return to a productive society, *Come With Me Now, Awake!* is the beginning of a discussion about restoring American innovation and entrepreneurship. Brown shows us how one alert person in a sea of sleepers can sound the alarm that wakes the world.

1. About the Author

Alice Elliott Brown blogs about how to attain good health, paid bills, a happy family, and inner peace. She is a former software executive, a Harvard MBA, and a committed herbalist. She doesn't really grasp the wisdom of posting her picture on the Internet.

Find Books by Alice Elliott Brown at:

2. www.AliceElliottBrown.com

Follow her blog on: AliceElliottBrown.wordpress.com

3. Join us to discuss good health, paid bills, a happy family, and inner peace.

www.ingramcontent.com/pod-product-compliance
Lightning Source LLC
Chambersburg PA
CBHW080720220326
41520CB00056B/7178